D0838207

Case Studies
in
Child and Adolescent
Psychopathology

Case Studies in Child and Adolescent Psychopathology

Robin K. Morgan
Indiana University Southeast

Prentice Hall, Upper Saddle River, New Jersey 07458

Library of Congress Cataloging-in-Publication Data

MORGAN, ROBIN K., (date)
    Case studies in child and adolescent psychopathology / Robin K. Morgan
        p.   cm.
    Includes bibliographical references and index.
    ISBN 0-13-079604-2
    1. Child psychopathology—Case studies.   2. Adolescent psychopathology—Case studies.   I. Title.
RJ499.M658   1999
618.92'89—dc21   98-27727
CIP

Editor in Chief: *Nancy Roberts*
Executive Editor: *Bill Webber*
Acquisition Editor: *Jennifer Gilliland*
Editorial Assistant: *Anita Castro*
Managing Editor: *Bonnie Biller*
Production Liaison: *Fran Russello*
Editorial / Production Supervision: *Kim Gueterman*
Prepress and Manufacturing Buyer: *Lynn Pearlman*
Cover Director: *Jayne Conte*
Cover Designer: *Bruce Kenselaar*
Copyeditor: *Kathryn Beck*

This book was set in 10 / 12 Palatino by The Composing Room of Michigan, Inc.
and was printed and bound by Courier Companies, Inc.
The cover was printed by Phoenix Color Corp.

© 1999 by Prentice-Hall, Inc.
A Pearson Education Company
Upper Saddle River, NJ 07458

All rights reserved. No part of this book may be
reproduced, in any form or by any means,
without permission in writing from the publisher.

Printed in the United States of America
10 9   8   7   6   5

ISBN 0-13-079604-2

Prentice-Hall International (UK) Limited,London
Prentice-Hall of Australia Pty. Limited, Sydney
Prentice-Hall Canada Inc., Toronto
Prentice-Hall Hispanoamericana, S.A., Mexico
Prentice-Hall of India Private Limited, New Delhi
Prentice-Hall of Japan, Inc., Tokyo
Pearson Education Asia Pte. Ltd., Singapore
Editora Prentice-Hall do Brasil, Ltda., Rio de Janeiro

For my husband,
who continues to believe in me
and accepts me for who I am

Contents

Section 2
DIAGNOSIS AND CONCEPTUALIZATION

Preface

Many case study books exist for courses in abnormal psychology. However, these texts typically focus on adults diagnosed with various disorders. Instructors teaching courses on child and adolescent psychopathology are limited in their options when selecting cases. These instructors may utilize case vignettes included in their textbook, they may use a casebook designed for general courses on psychopathology, or they may attempt to find a casebook that deals exclusively with children and adolescents. Unfortunately, the first option is rarely acceptable because cases in the textbooks are usually brief and fragmented, preventing students from gaining a clear understanding of the disordered life of the individual. The second option, selecting a case study book that was meant for a more general course in adult psychopathology, is equally frustrating. Although many of the more general case study books do include cases involving children or adolescents, these represent only about 15 percent of the cases presented. Obviously, this is not an ideal solution for the instructor. Finally, the instructor may select the third option and attempt to find a case book that deals exclusively with child and adolescent disorders. This search will be long and arduous, for few such case study books exist.

While helping to fill this void, this casebook fulfills two main goals: (1) to provide detailed descriptions of a range of clinical problems affecting children and adolescents, and (2) to illustrate some of the ways these problems can be examined and treated. At the same time, this text also responds to another need that demands its existence: as with most child and adolescent disorders, symptoms and associated features of the disorder may be quite different, at times even seemingly opposite, of symptons presented by adults.

In selecting cases for the book, an attempt was made to present "classic" symptoms and problematic issues. The social context in which the symptoms occur have also been stressed even when these social factors are not directly related to diagnosis. This inclusion is valuable because as is well known the disorders of children and adolescents often involve social influences from family, school, or other environments that often contribute to or reinforce the disorder exhibited by the child or adolescent. It is important that students begin to understand that these factors may be critical in determining a person's overall adjustment.

In this casebook, all diagnoses are made utilizing the most recent criteria established in the *Diagnostic and Statistical Manual of Mental Disorders* of the American Psychiatric Association (DSM-IV, 1994). Appropriate for upper-level undergraduates as well as beginning graduate students in child and adolescent psychopathology courses, this casebook may also be included in courses in psychiatric social work, nursing, and counseling, and ultimately could serve as a reference tool for all professionals in the above fields.

Every case in this book is based on actual clinical experience, primarily that of the author, but in some instances, that of colleagues and students. Various demographic characteristics (names, locations, and occupations) and some concrete clinical details have been changed to ensure the anonymity of clients and their families. In some instances, the cases are composites of clinical problems with which the author has dealt. The intent is not to claim efficacy and utility for any particular conceptualization, but rather to illustrate some of the ways clinicians think about and attempt to treat such problems. The names used in the case studies are fictitious; any resemblance to actual persons is purely coincidental.

The casebook is organized into two sections. The first section includes case studies along with space for students to write their ideas about diagnosis and treatment. The second section includes the diagnosis made by the therapist in the case, the rationale behind the diagnosis, and treatment considerations. This separation is used to allow students to work on the cases prior to uncovering how the "experts" viewed the case. Hopefully, this pedagogical technique will encourage the students to think through the issues on their own rather than just turning to the "correct answer."

Finally, I would like to thank the following individuals for their helpful comments: Bill Sweigart, Indiana University Southeast; Amanda Bergstedt, Indiana University Southeast; Mary Anne Baker, Indiana University Southeast; David Morgan, Spalding University, and Leonard Doerfler, Assumption College. I am also grateful to those who reviwed my book: Bente K. Fischer, Jane Gaultney of the University of North Carolina—Charlotte, and Eric Cooley of Western Oregon University. In addition, I would like to thank my children, Sarah and Zachary, for their daily smiles and hugs which cheered me on even when the writing process was at its most difficult stages.

Robin K. Morgan
New Albany, IN

Case Studies
in
Child and Adolescent
Psychopathology

Section 1
CASE STUDIES

CASE **1**   *Natasha*

Natasha Reed's name was placed on the list of children in need of evaluation by her third-grade teacher. In the Greene County educational system, teachers could recommend children for intellectual and emotional evaluations if they had any concerns. As a result, Natasha would be evaluated by a psychologist employed by the school. Natasha was brought to the testing center by her parents.

Natasha was a nine-year, six-month-old Caucasian female with short brown hair who was of average height and weight. Natasha was the youngest child from an intact family of four children. Her oldest brother (age fifteen) as well as her two older sisters (ages thirteen and eleven), were described by the mother as good students, typically earning As and Bs in school. The mother reported no pregnancy or birth complications with Natasha. Natasha had been a healthy and happy child who was easy to care for and manage, although she seemed to lag consistently a year or more behind her brother and sisters in language acquisition, toilet training, self-help, and play activities. As an example, Natasha did not learn to dress herself until she was five, and, at nine, she was still unable to tie her own shoes.

The parents appeared to be open and honest with each other and strongly committed to family-type activities such as church and sports. Both parents have completed college and are employed. Mr. Reed is employed as a computer programmer at the local university, where he has been employed for the past eighteen years. Mrs. Reed returned to work when Natasha was three and has been employed as a social worker by the local Department of Child Welfare.

Natasha began preschool when she was three. The parents reported that Natasha had attended preschool with no difficulties. Natasha liked other children and played well with both girls and boys. Natasha had remained at the same preschool for three years on the advice of the teacher. Natasha had a birthday in late August which would have made her the youngest child in kindergarten. Therefore, given her birthday and her general slowness to develop, Natasha had stayed in preschool. At six, Natasha began kindergarten. Kindergarten was a pleasant, stimulating experience for Natasha. School

1

records suggested that Natasha was cooperative, friendly, and willing to share with the other children. It was noted, however, that since Natasha scored low on a reading readiness test, she might have difficulty with reading in first grade. As predicted, Natasha had difficulty learning to read in the first grade. By the end of first grade, Natasha could sound out only a few words. Despite daily tutoring sessions in the second grade, Natasha continued to lag behind her classmates in reading. Now, in the third grade, Natasha could read only the most simple of books (approximately a first-grade reading level), while her classmates were reading chapter books. According to Natasha's teacher, many of the other children were beginning to make fun of Natasha and to call her names.

Natasha was administered the Wechsler Intelligence Scale for Children–Revised (WISC-R), the Wide-Range Achievement Test (WRAT), the Bender-Gestalt, and the Adaptive Behavior Inventory for Children. On the WISC-R, Natasha earned a Verbal Scale IQ score of 65, a Performance Scale IQ score of 64, and a Full Scale IQ Score of 65. On the WRAT, Natasha scored in the 6th percentile in Reading and the 4th percentile in Arithmetic. Results of the Bender-Gestalt were in the 6th percentile, Koppitz score. The Adaptive Behavior Inventory for Children confirmed the more general comments of Natasha's parents and teachers. Natasha was able to score well on those items reflecting cooperation with others but scored two years younger than her chronological age on items reflecting physical skills.

Possible Diagnosis and Treatment Options

CASE 2   *Joey*

Mr. and Mrs. Bowen were met in the waiting room by the therapist. Mr. Bowen was a short, overweight Caucasian man in his late twenties dressed in dark work pants and a lighter work shirt of the same color. Mrs. Bowen was also slightly overweight but stood a good 6 inches taller than her husband. She was dressed casually but neatly in dress slacks and blouse. Joey, their four year-old-son, was sitting on the floor midway between his mother and father.

While an associate stayed with Joey, the Bowens were interviewed by the therapist. The Bowens reported that they had called the therapist out of frustration when their son, Joey, had been "kicked out" of preschool the previous week. According to the Bowens, Joey's teacher had called daily since preschool started three weeks ago with complaints about their son. The teacher, Ms. Small, complained that Joey did not interact with the other children but simply sat on the floor and stared, would not talk, and would hit any child who touched him. All attempts to engage Joey in singing, painting, or other activities failed. If the teacher insisted that Joey participate, Joey would sit on the floor and have a "temper tantrum." These tantrums consisted of screaming, crying, and banging his arms and legs against the floor. Mrs. Bowen reported that these temper tantrums occurred at home as well as at preschool.

Mrs. Bowen, through tears, reported that Joey hated to be touched, even at home, and would frequently hit her if she tried to hug him. Joey spent most of his time at home sitting on the floor of his room. Mrs. Bowen reported that he had never liked playing with other children and rarely, if ever, talked.

The therapist asked what Joey's physician had said about Joey's behavior. Mrs. Bowen reported that their insurance only paid for hospital visits and Joey received his immunization shots through a clinic. She went on to report that the nurse had thought Joey might be deaf when he was two but tests had revealed he had normal vision and hearing. The nurse had reassured the Bowens that children developed at different ages and Joey should begin talking soon. Mr. Bowen commented that two years had passed and Joey still didn't talk. Mrs. Bowen patted her husband on his knee before stating that when they had taken Joey back to the clinic about six months later, the nurse had suggested they see a psychologist, as she thought Joey might be mentally retarded.

Upon further questioning, the Bowens revealed that Joey was their first —and, so far—only child. They had been surprised that Joey did not like to be held or cuddled. He would scream when Mrs. Bowen tried to rock him to sleep. Whereas other babies began smiling at their parents at about three to four months of age, Joey never smiled at his parents. Other than temper tantrums, Joey rarely showed any emotion. Mrs. Bowen reported that since Joey was about seven months old, he would frequently bang his head against the side of his crib or his wall. When she or her husband would hold him to prevent his injuring himself, Joey would try to bite them and kick them. Mr. Bowen reported that at these times, Joey was extremely strong and frequently left bruises on his or his wife's arms and legs.

Further questioning revealed that Mrs. Bowen experienced no difficulties during her pregnancy, not even morning sickness. Joey was born two days before his due date and weighed a little over 8 pounds. Joey had suffered two ear infections since his birth and had chicken pox when he was three. Other than normal colds, Joey had not been seriously ill.

Joey had potty-trained himself. One morning when Joey was about three, Mrs. Bowen had gone to his room to change his diaper and had found Joey sitting on the toilet in the bathroom. Since this day, Joey wore underpants and had managed to have only two accidents, both while he was having a tantrum. While potty-training had been easy, getting Joey to sleep and eat was not. Mrs. Bowen reported that Joey slept fitfully. While he was usually in bed and asleep by 8 P.M., he frequently awoke his parents around midnight with his head banging. He fell back asleep around 1 A.M. and would get up and wander around the house at 4 or 5 A.M. Mr. Bowen admitted that he had taken to locking Joey's door at night to prevent him from being injured. Eating was another problem area. Joey refused to eat any foods that were green or red. As long as the foods were not green or red, Joey would eat. If there was a single speck of green or red, Joey would throw the food onto the floor and scream.

When asked how Joey's behavior affected the Bowens, Mrs. Bowen began crying. Mr. Bowen glanced at his wife helplessly before responding that he and his wife had thought about a trial separation the previous summer. However, they had decided against it as they realized they loved each other. Mr. Bowen went on to talk about how frustrated he was with Joey and how angry he became when Joey had a tantrum. Mrs. Bowen commented that she had wanted three children but feared having another child with problems like Joey's.

After the Bowens were calm, Joey was brought into the room. Joey was a slight, blond-haired boy of four years of age. He walked into the room and sat in the middle of the floor without glancing at the therapist or his parents. He ignored all questions from his parents and the therapist. When the therapist handed him a doll, Joey began rocking back and forth without touching the doll. The therapist removed the doll and laid a children's book on the floor next to Joey. Joey continued rocking apparently unaware of the book. When the therapist reached to take the book, Joey grabbed the book and began rocking faster while clutching the book. As he rocked, a guttural sound began to come from Joey. Despite repeated attempts to engage Joey, no further progress was made.

It was decided that Joey would return in three days for a thorough assessment. The parents also agreed to take Joey to see a pediatrician to rule out medical problems and to allow the therapist to talk with Joey's preschool teacher. When the parents got up to leave, Joey also stood, clutching the children's book. Mrs. Bowen told Joey to return the book to the therapist. Joey once again began rocking and making a guttural noise. At this point the therapist knelt in front of Joey and asked him, "Read book?" Joey sat on the floor and handed the therapist the book. Astonished, the parents sank into their chair while the therapist read the book to Joey. While the therapist read, Joey rocked back and forth. When the therapist finished reading the book, Joey stood and walked toward the door.

Possible Diagnosis and Treatment Options

CASE 3   *Jimmy*

Jimmy's mother, Mrs. Conner, called the therapist's office in tears. She and her husband had attended the first parent-teacher conference of the year for their son. At the conference, Jimmy's teacher, Ms. Hall, had recommended that Jimmy be immediately placed on Ritalin as his hyperactivity was disturbing the class. Mrs. Conner had called her pediatrician, who had given her the therapist's name and number. The therapist scheduled a meeting with the parents for that afternoon.

Mr. and Mrs. Conner were in their late twenties. Mr. Conner wore a uniform of a local factory. Mrs. Conner was dressed neatly in a skirt and blouse, her eyes red-rimmed and swollen.

Mr. Conner began the conversation by asking why he and his wife were being seen when Jimmy was the one misbehaving in class. The therapist explained that at this point it was unclear what was occurring in the classroom to upset the teacher. The parents were being seen first to provide background information and to provide consent for the therapist to observe Jimmy's behavior in the classroom, and to speak with Jimmy's teacher. In addition, the therapist described situations in which a child's behavior can be improved by working with the parents, rather than the child. The Conners appeared to be relieved by the therapist's explanation.

Mr. Conner reported that he had worked in the factory since he graduated from high school. Although he made good money, he frequently worked overtime, including weekends and holidays. Mrs. Conner, therefore, had primary responsibility for the children. Jimmy, aged seven, and the only boy, was the eldest of three children. His twin sisters, aged five, were currently in preschool and were doing well.

Mrs. Conner reported that Jimmy was an active child who was always running around the house and crashing into the furniture. She stated that he had walked early, at ten months, and had been keeping her running ever since. All other developmental milestones were reported as occurring within a normal range. His favorite show was *Power Rangers*, during which he would act out the moves of the characters. Jimmy did not like anyone to read to him. Jimmy preferred riding his bike and playing with his trucks and cars.

In preschool, Jimmy had difficulty adjusting. The teacher had reported that Jimmy did not sit still and would not be quiet. Because of these problems, Mrs. Conner had taken Jimmy out of preschool and kept him at home. In kindergarten, Jimmy again had difficulty obeying instructions, but Mrs. Conner attributed these problems to his not attending preschool. The kindergarten teacher was also confident that Jimmy would eventually settle down and learn the routine.

This year Jimmy entered the first grade. The Conners had been hopeful that things were going well as they had not received any notes or calls from the teacher. They were surprised when the teacher was so upset at the conference the night before.

Mr. Conner stated that he believed Jimmy's problem was that he "needed a good spanking." Jimmy was being allowed to disrupt the class and the teachers just didn't punish him. Mr. Conner reported that his wife was "too easy" on the kids. He went on to report that if he had acted the way Jimmy was acting in school he would have "gotten a beating."

After much discussion, the Conners agreed not to spank or otherwise discipline Jimmy over the problems at school until the therapist had a chance to observe Jimmy, and do a thorough assessment. At this point the therapist had the parents sign the proper papers, and a time was set for the Conners to bring Jimmy in for testing. The parents were given checklists to complete, describing Jimmy's typical behavior in the home. When returned, these checklists confirmed the Conners's self-reports and indicated that Jimmy never sat through an entire television show. Even when his favorite show, *Power Rangers*, was playing, Jimmy would sit for only two to three minutes before he began jumping around the room.

The therapist contacted the teacher and arranged to meet with her before school to discuss Jimmy's behavior. Ms. Hall met with the therapist in her classroom. Ms. Hall reported that she was pleased that the Conners had contacted a therapist but believed Jimmy needed to be on Ritalin. She described Jimmy as a complete disruption to the class. He was constantly out of his chair, blurted out answers without waiting to be called upon, bothered the other children when they were working, and failed to complete his assignments. When asked about Jimmy's positive qualities, Ms. Hall appeared confused. Finally, she stated that most of the children liked Jimmy and he seemed to be a natural leader. In addition, he had been chosen to play the lead in the first-grade play because he was able to speak clearly and was quite engaging. When asked about academic performance, Ms. Hall opened a file folder on her desk containing Jimmy's work from the first nine weeks of school. As the therapist scanned the work, it quickly became apparent that Jimmy's work was inconsistent. Some papers had not been completed, others had received a perfect grade.

Ms. Hall agreed to complete a checklist describing Jimmy's typical behavior in the classroom. She also agreed to the therapist's sitting in the back of the classroom to observe Jimmy's behavior.

The therapist moved to the back of the class and watched the children come in the room. In the general confusion of putting away coats and bookbags, Jimmy's behavior was not abnormal. Jimmy was of average height and weight for his age. He had curly brown hair and wore jeans, sneakers, and a t-shirt with the name of a local college. After putting his jacket and bookbag away, Jimmy moved around the classroom, checking on the fish and the hamster, looking out the window, and glancing at the therapist. The therapist was careful not to observe Jimmy directly.

After the bell rang, Ms. Hall asked all of the children to take their seats. All did, except Jimmy. Jimmy continued to wander about the room until Ms. Hall directly asked him to sit down. Once seated, Jimmy bounced up and down in his seat and tapped his pencil on the desktop. When asked to read, Jimmy jumped up and read the passage requested while swaying back and forth. His reading was quite good. Upon reseating, Jimmy took all of his books out of his desk and put them on the floor. He then started talking to the child behind him until Ms. Hall asked him to stop. Jimmy got up from his desk and went over to stare at the fish. Ms. Hall once again told Jimmy to sit down, which he did. The other children giggled when Jimmy was reprimanded by Ms. Hall. The rest of the morning continued along the same vein. By the time the students went to Music, the therapist was exhausted.

Ms. Hall confirmed that the morning had been a typical one. The therapist asked Ms. Hall if Jimmy might be bored in the classroom. She stated that she was unsure and had never considered that. The therapist assured the teacher he would keep her informed of his progress in dealing with Jimmy.

Jimmy arrived for his testing session with the therapist dressed in much the same way as he had been at school. Jimmy's face lit up when he saw the therapist and commented on his being in Jimmy's classroom the previous week. Jimmy reported that he knew his parents and his teacher were mad at him for being so "bad." When questioned about his behavior, Jimmy reported that he knew he was supposed to sit still but that he couldn't. He reported that his favorite subject was lunch and his least favorite was math. Jimmy reported that he liked the other children and was happy that he had such a large part in the play. He described his sisters in fairly positive terms except that he called them "spoilt brats." When directly questioned about his parents, he reported that he wished his dad was around more and that his mom wouldn't get so angry with him all the time.

After the interview, Jimmy was given the Wechsler Intelligence Scale for Children–Revised, a Sentence Completion Test, and the Bender-Gestalt. Overall, his score on the WISC-R was 121 with a Verbal score of 128, and a Performance score of 116. While his overall score was good, Jimmy showed variability in the subtests reflective of his complaints and inattention. He complained vehemently during the mathematical portions of the test. In addition, he frequently got out of his seat and walked around the room. The therapist had to repeatedly bring him back to the task at hand. The Bender-Gestalt results were age-appropriate. The Sentence Completion task showed no significant concerns other than what might be expected for a child of Jimmy's age.

Possible Diagnosis and Treatment Options

CASE 4 *Randall*

The interviewer was first made aware of Randall Ellis while attending a workshop. A school psychologist approached the interviewer and described Randall, aged twelve, who was presently in the sixth grade at a local elementary school. He had been diagnosed with Attention Deficit Hyperactivity Disorder in the second grade and had been taking Ritalin since that time. According to the school psychologist, Randall was on the verge of being suspended from school because of his inappropriate behavior. The school psychologist was hopeful the interviewer might be willing to assess Randall to determine if Randall had other psychological difficulties in addition to the ADHD. The school psychologist reported being comfortable assessing school-related problems but believed Randall's problems required more expertise in assessing psychopathology. The interviewer agreed to see Randall if his parents so desired.

The following week the interviewer received a call from Randall's mother, Mrs. Ellis. Mrs. Ellis expressed her frustration with Randall and directly asked whether bringing Randall to another therapist was ". . . going to do any good?" The interviewer told Mrs. Ellis that all that could be promised was a complete evaluation. At the end of the evaluation, the interviewer would be able to answer her questions more thoroughly. Mrs. Ellis agreed to the consultation, made an appointment for Randall, and authorized the therapist to observe Randall in school.

On the following morning, the interviewer went to Randall's school. School records confirmed the school psychologist's report. Randall had attended the elementary school since kindergarten. His behavior in kindergarten and first grade was characterized by his teachers as extremely immature. Randall was described as being constantly out of his seat, rude to his teachers, and impulsive. Randall did not wait to be called upon but simply shouted out answers. In music class, he held his hands over his ears and complained that the music was too loud. His interactions with other children were also described as problematic. Randall called other children names, pushed them, and would take their money from their desks.

In second grade, Randall's physician, at the request of his parents and his teacher, diagnosed Randall as having ADHD and placed him on Ritalin. Other than during the summer, Randall had been on Ritalin since that time. Teachers had reported that Randall was calmer when he was taking his Ritalin but that he continued to demonstrate inappropriate behaviors such as stealing, lying, being disrespectful to the teachers, hitting other children, and disrupting the class by passing gas, pounding his head on the desk or wall, and talking loudly.

Randall's academic performance was also problematic. While standardized tests revealed that Randall had an above average level of intelligence (117 on the Cognitive Skills Index, a test frequently used by the local elementary schools to estimate level of intelligence), he typically earned Cs and Ds in his classes. He was always promoted from one year to the next, but teachers expressed concern about the discrepancy between his performance and his level of ability.

The interviewer sat in the back of Randall's class during the class period before lunch. During lunch and recess, the interviewer observed Randall from a distance while pretending to interact with the lunchroom monitors and then the playground monitors. Randall was below average height but slightly overweight. He was the only child in the room of Asian descent. He was dressed in jeans, a t-shirt, and sneakers in a manner similar to that of the other children in the class.

In the classroom, Randall was off-task for the entire forty-minute period. While the other students were answering questions or listening to the teacher, Randall banged his head on his desk, poked the student in front of him with a pencil, and repeatedly passed gas. The teacher ignored Randall's misbehavior for the most part. When Randall passed gas, the teacher commented, "Let's all get our gas masks out!" The child in front of Randall told Randall to stop poking her. When this happened, the teacher told the girl she would receive a discipline card if she did not stop talking in class.

At lunch, Randall continued to behave inappropriately. He made rude comments about the food to the children sitting around him, attempted to put french fries down one girl's t-shirt, and was eating with his mouth open. When the girl told Randall not to touch her, several other students yelled at Randall. Randall responded to their yells by sitting quietly for several minutes.

Recess showed a continuation of this pattern. Randall chased girls around the playground and knocked one girl to the ground twice. Children who reported Randall's misbehavior to the teachers or to the playground monitors were told to leave him alone. When Randall's behavior became enough of an irritant, the other children would yell at him or tell him that they, or their parent, would beat him up if he did not stop. The childrens' approach halted Randall's behavior for approximately two to five minutes.

On the following day, Randall and his parents came to see the interviewer. Randall waited in a playroom while the interviewer met with his parents. Mrs. Ellis was a small woman of Asian descent dressed casually in a denim skirt and blouse. Mr. Ellis was a large man dressed in jeans and a polo shirt. Mr. Ellis was Caucasian.

The Ellises reported that Randall was Mrs. Ellis's child by a previous marriage. She had divorced Randall's father when Randall was six months old. Mr. Ellis had adopted Randall when he was fourteen months after marrying Randall's mother. Mr. Ellis was the only father Randall had ever known. According to Mrs. Ellis, she and her first husband were both Korean and had come to the United States with their parents during the Korean War in the 1950s. After the birth of Randall, her husband had returned to Korea to work. She had refused to leave the United States, leading to their divorce. Randall's biological father refused to have anything to do with his son, claiming that the child wasn't his because he was too "Americanized."

The Ellises had three additional children, aged nine, seven, and four. No problems were reported with the other three children. Mrs. Ellis reported that she believed in mothers remaining home while their children were small. She hoped to return to college and pursue a degree in sociology once her youngest was in first grade. Mr. Ellis worked with his family on their farm. The farm was a large one, over 1,000 acres, and was open to the public for picking strawberries, blackberries, apples, peaches, and pumpkins.

The Ellises reported that Randall had been an easy baby with no medical or behavioral problems during his first two years. All developmental milestones were achieved within normal limits. They began to notice how "stubborn" Randall was shortly after his second birthday. They attributed this to the "terrible twos" and tried not to punish him for hitting other children or throwing temper tantrums when he was denied a toy or treat. Randall's behavior did not improve when he turned three or four. When Randall began kindergarten, his teacher expressed concern about Randall's behavior and suggested that he stay in kindergarten for two years to "mature." The Ellises were concerned that Randall would be made fun of and sent him to the first grade. The Ellises stated that the same type of behavioral problems were reported by Randall's first-grade teacher and that Randall continued to disobey at home, often hitting his siblings when Mr. and Mrs. Ellis were not watching. When questioned about his misbehavior, Randall would lie, even though his parents had observed him engaging in the misbehavior.

When questioned, the Ellises reported that they spanked Randall once for each lie and twice for each time he hit another child. Mr. Ellis administered all spankings because Randall would laugh and tell his mother that her spankings did not hurt him.

The Ellises reported that Randall did not sleep as much as their other children except when he was taken off the Ritalin during the summer. No problems with appetite were noted. No other problems, including developmental, were noted, although Mrs. Ellis reported that Randall was physically awkward, leading to his being unable to perform well in sports. She noted that he still occasionally fell off his bicycle or ran into parked cars or trees.

Randall was seen by the interviewer immediately following completion of the parents' interview. Although compliant, Randall frequently rolled his eyes when the interviewer asked a question. Randall reported that he knew his parents were upset with him for "being bad" but that it wasn't his fault because he had ADHD. He explained that his ADHD caused him all sorts of problems and that he shouldn't be penalized because he was sick. He reported that hitting the other children, pharting, and talking loudly were all because of his ADHD and that his Ritalin just wasn't strong enough to control all of his illness. He commented that his behavior was much worse when he forgot to take his medicine.

Randall reported that he disliked school and found most of his teachers boring. He stated that teasing girls was "a lot of fun" because they would squeal. He enjoyed getting the other children, especially girls, in trouble and didn't really mind getting in trouble himself if one of the girls also got in trouble. He reported that the school never really followed their own rules. He explained that they had repeatedly told him that he would be expelled if he caused additional problems, but that they never kicked him out for good.

When questioned, Randall reported that he enjoyed reading about motorcycles and race cars and would like to attend a race someday like the Indianapolis 500. He reported that the only school subject he liked was English. Randall reported that he had several friends in his neighborhood, including two boys with whom he would catch stray cats. When questioned about what he did with these cats, Randall replied "nothing."

Randall was administered the Wechsler Scale of Intelligence for Children, a Wide-Range Achievement Test, and the Bender-Gestalt. His performance on the Bender-Gestalt was normal for his age. The Wide-Range Achievement Test confirmed his teachers' reports of his poor academic performance; he scored in the 77th percentile for Reading, the 50th percentile for Spelling, and the 45th percentile for Arithmetic. His relatively high reading score corresponded with Randall's own comments about liking English and how he enjoyed reading about certain topics.

On the Wechsler scale, Randall scored in the above average range on the Verbal Scale (125), and average on the Performance Scale (108). His Full Scale IQ of 115 placed him in the above average range of intellectual functioning, which corresponded well with the school's estimate of his intellectual functioning.

Possible Diagnosis and Treatment Options

CASE 5　　　*Scott*

Scott first met the therapist in the hall of the local elementary school. The therapist was leaving the school after assessing a child when Scott was brought down the hallway. Scott attempted to trip the therapist as he walked past. Scott's teacher jerked Scott into the principal's office and the therapist followed. Scott was a biracial child of an African American mother and Caucasian father. His parents had divorced when Scott was six and Scott's father had received full custody. Now ten, Scott was brought to the office as a result of setting a fire in the schoolyard.

According to the principal, Scott was a fourth grader. While he performed well on the yearly assessments, Scott was a terror in the classroom. He refused to stay in his seat, talked whenever he wanted, made rude comments to his teacher and the other children, and hit any child who refused to give him money upon demand. The previous week, Scott had set a fire in the schoolyard. Even though no damage had been done, the school insisted on pressing charges.

At this point, the therapist asked permission to help with the case. After discussion with all parties, the school agreed not to press charges if Scott were sent to the therapist.

The therapist met with Scott, his father, and his stepmother the following day. Scott's father, Mr. Bridges, had remarried the year after his divorce. He and his present wife had twin boys, aged two, and another child on the way. The second Mrs. Bridges was Caucasian.

Mr. Bridges reported that Scott had always been a difficult child in that he asked so many questions. Frequently Mr. Bridges would get so tired of Scott's questions that he would send him to his room to get a break. Mr. Bridges reported that his first wife became an alcoholic when Scott was four, leading to their subsequent divorce. Mr. Bridges denied any alcohol use on the part of the mother during pregnancy. Developmental milestones were reached by Scott within a normal range.

Mr. Bridges reported that Scott attended daycare from the time he was six weeks old and no problems were noted. His kindergarten teachers described him as an active, bright, mischievous boy. It was during the first grade that the divorce occurred. After the divorce, his first-grade teacher reported that Scott was having trouble getting along with the other children. By second grade, teachers reported that Scott was becoming rude and would not obey orders. By third grade, Scott began taking money from the other children and hitting them when they protested. The present school year had seen a continuation and escalation of these difficulties until the current fire-setting episode. In the past six months, Scott had run away from home on two occasions. The first time, he returned on his own by breakfast. On the second occasion, he was gone two days before he was found by his father.

Mr. Bridges reported that he was frustrated with Scott and was ready to ship him off to a boarding school if he didn't improve. Mrs. Bridges asked if this might be best for Scott given the young children in the household.

When questioned, Mr. Bridges reported that the court awarded him custody because his ex-wife was an alcoholic. In fact, his ex-wife had recently been diagnosed as HIV-positive. Mr. Bridges described his first marriage as a "stupid mistake" and an "incident in his life best forgotten." Mr. Bridges is employed as an accountant and Mrs. Bridges remains at home to care for the children.

Mrs. Bridges reported that she never felt close to Scott. Even as a six-year-old, he had been questioning of authority figures and "insensitive" to her feelings. In addition, she reported that Scott consistently lies to her. She described Scott as a "budding con-man" who lies to avoid chores and homework. She expressed considerable concern that he would injure the twins or the new baby.

After questioning Mr. and Mrs. Bridges, Scott was brought into the room to be interviewed alone. Despite his surliness and rudeness throughout the interview, the therapist was impressed by Scott's intelligence and pain. Scott reported that his parents didn't care about him and he was glad because he didn't care about them either. He referred to his stepmother as "Wonder Bread" and his father as a "wimp." He refused to talk about his birth mother other than to say that if she loved him, she wouldn't have left him with "Wonder Bread and the wimp."

Scott reported that school was "a joke," given that all the classes were too easy. He also stated that he disliked his school, as he was the only "black" person there. He commented that all he had to do was act tough and the students caved in because they were "scared of blacks."

When asked why Scott had tried to trip the therapist, Scott finally responded that he thought it might be funny to see a "white guy licking my feet." Scott also reported that setting the fire was an accident; he just enjoyed watching fire. However, as he talked, his eyes lit up as he described how the fire had spread.

After meeting with Mr. and Mrs. Bridges, the therapist contacted Scott's teacher. The teacher confirmed the misbehavior reported in the office, by his parents, and by Scott. Interestingly enough, Scott's teacher was Asian. She commented that she believed Scott felt isolated because of his race, but she pointed out that two children in Scott's class were Hispanic.

Possible Diagnosis and Treatment Options

CASE 6   *Eric*

Eric, aged eight, was brought to the clinic by his parents who were quite concerned about his behavior. The parents were insistent that they speak with the clinician first while Eric played in the waiting room. Eric's mother, an overweight woman of approximately thirty years of age, was dressed casually but neatly. Eric's father, a tall, lean man of about the same age as his wife, was also dressed in casual clothes but apologized profusely for his appearance, stating that they had just come from a softball game. Eric's mother answered most of the examiner's questions, while his father nodded in agreement and provided additional information only when directly asked.

Eric's mother blushed as she confessed that Eric repeatedly soiled his pants. Over the past six months, Eric had defecated in his pants at home and at school approximately once a week. Over the past week, the "accidents" had increased in frequency to approximately once a day. Eric's mother described Eric as a normal baby who slept through the night from the day they brought him home from the hospital. He walked by thirteen months of age and was completely potty-trained by twenty-eight months. No toileting accidents were reported until the past six months.

Eric is an only child whose mother works as an elementary school teacher and whose father works as an accountant. While both parents had wanted at least three children, Eric's mother is unable to have additional children. Eric's parents described their marriage as happy and could not identify any stressful incident occurring within the past year.

Eric is in the second grade at a local public school where he earns all As. In fact, Eric is such a good reader that he is allowed to read with the third-grade class. Although Eric has never been overly popular with his classmates, he has two good friends in his class with whom he has spent the night. According to Eric's parents, his friends have continued to play with him despite his "accidents" at home and at school. Eric's father, however, is concerned that if Eric does not stop this behavior the other children will tease him.

Eric entered the therapy room alone. His parents insisted that the clinician speak with Eric without the parents in the room. Eric is a slight boy with thick brown hair covering his brow. He carried a book in one hand. Once seated, he placed the book on his lap and waited patiently for the clinician to begin.

When questioned, Eric described his life as very happy except that he never had time to read. Eric reported that his parents always want him to go outside and play, without his books. He stated that his two best friends also enjoy reading and pretending to be pirates. Eric reported that he enjoys school except for some kids who always tease him on the bus. He simply ignores them and reads his book instead.

When asked about the "accidents," Eric squirmed in his chair and reported that his parents were pretty upset with him. Eric explained that on each occasion he was either reading or playing pirates and didn't want to stop to go to the bathroom. He kept thinking, "just one more minute," until it was too late. He reported that he really didn't mind except his parents were upset and that he didn't want to lose his friends. When asked why he never urinated in his pants, Eric grimaced and said, "Yuck, that's gross!"

Possible Diagnosis and Treatment Options

CASE 7   *Sam*

Sam Jeffries was brought to the community mental health center by his parents. Mr. and Mrs. Jeffries met with the therapist while Sam waited in another room.

According to his parents, Sam had been acting in a "bizarre" manner for the past three months. Mrs. Jeffries reported that she had an uncle who was hospitalized for schizophrenia and was concerned that Sam had the same disorder. Sam was described as a wonderful baby who slept through the night almost immediately. He was easy to care for and allowed his parents to take him anywhere. As a toddler, Sam was very clean and organized. He disliked getting dirt on his clothing or shoes and would spend hours organizing his toys.

When Sam went to preschool the teacher described him as a "perfect gentleman." Early elementary school teachers had also told Mr. and Mrs. Jeffries how neat and well-organized their son was. Mrs. Jeffries reported that she and her husband had always seen this as a positive attribute until the past few months. This year Sam had entered the ninth grade, his first year in high school. Since the beginning of school, Sam had developed noticeable facial tics and had been taking longer and longer to complete his homework. At first, the Jefferies believed Sam was just being given more homework in high school, but then they had begun receiving notes from his teachers complaining that Sam never turned in assignments.

When questioned, Mrs. Jeffries reported that Sam reached his home about 3:30 each afternoon and worked until 11 P.M. each night on his homework. His only break during this time was for dinner from 6 to 6:30. On the weekends, Sam would arise at 7 A.M. and work all day until his parents forced him to go to bed. Despite these long hours, Sam's grades, mostly Cs, were the worst he had ever received.

Mr. and Mrs. Jeffries reported that Sam was an only child and had no serious medical problems. While Mr. Jeffries worked for a local bank, Mrs. Jeffries was a teacher and was home each day by the time Sam reached home.

After returning the parents to the waiting room, Sam followed the therapist back to the office. Sam was a tall, lanky, fourteen-year-old Caucasian. He was dressed casually in blue jeans and polo shirt. He was cooperative throughout the interview, expressing interest in the room and exhibiting a wide range of knowledge about current events including music, sports, and politics. As indicated by his parents, Sam had a facial tic consisting of a facial grimace on the right side of his face. No other motor or vocal tics were observed.

Sam reported that he found high school to be much harder than elementary or junior high school. He also reported that his best friends in eighth grade were no longer his best friends in ninth grade. Though Sam was more interested in music, his old friends were more interested in dating and cars. He acknowledged that he had made a couple of new friends but that he didn't have as much time to devote to friendships as he did in the past.

When asked about his study habits, Sam's facial tic noticeably increased. Sam also began tapping his foot. He reported that he used to be able to complete his homework in a couple of hours but that it seemed to be taking him longer and longer to complete his assignments. When asked about the notes from his teachers stating that his assignments had not been turned in, Sam sighed and stated that he couldn't turn in messy work.

The therapist asked Sam to describe the process he went through in completing his assignments. Sam visibly relaxed as his voice took on a sing-song quality. Sam reported that he got five sheets of lined notepaper, five sheets of blank paper to use as scrap paper, three sharpened pencils, and his text. He lined everything up "just so" on his desk and began. When he made a mistake, he would start over because "neatness is most important." Sam reported that it was especially frustrating to start over when he had almost finished a long assignment. When asked why he couldn't just erase the error and continue on the same paper, Sam's facial tic and foot tapping began again, and he responded that he couldn't stand for things to be messy. When the therapist asked again how Sam would feel if he turned in a paper with an error on it, Sam became upset and stated that he "couldn't do such a thing."

Sam denied having eating problems or sleep problems. He reported that he frequently got an upset stomach when he felt he wasn't going to complete his assignments. Sam also reported that he was worried about doing well in school and making new friends.

Possible Diagnosis and Treatment Options

CASE **8**   *Amanda*

Amanda's mother, Mrs. Anderson, was defensive when she called the therapist for an appointment. Over the phone she informed the therapist that her husband insisted on Amanda being seen because he felt that Amanda was overly dependent on her mother. After much discussion, it was agreed that Amanda and both of her parents would be seen the following week.

When the therapist entered the waiting room, Amanda was sitting on her mother's lap while her father sat across the room looking at a magazine. After introductions were made the therapist asked to meet with Amanda privately. While agreeing, Mrs. Anderson gave her daughter several kisses and reassured her repeatedly that Amanda could run back to the waiting room if she became afraid. Although reluctant, Amanda agreed to leave with the therapist.

Amanda was a tall, stocky seven-year-old Caucasian with long blond hair. Her size was closer to that of a ten-year-old than an average seven-year-old. She wore a frilly pink dress, white socks, and black patent-leather shoes. Amanda carried a pink elephant purse and her Barbie.

Upon entering the therapist's office, she glanced around warily from the doorway before perching on the edge of the chair nearest the door. At first, Amanda answered only in monosyllables. After a few minutes of drawing, she began to talk more spontaneously.

Amanda reported that she lived with her mother and father in a new house in the country. Her maternal grandparents lived two houses down the street. Amanda stated that she was an only child but would like to have brothers and sisters because she was frequently lonely. Amanda currently attends first grade at the local public school. Prior to kindergarten, she had remained home with her mother or with her maternal grandmother. While other children live in the neighborhood, Amanda is not allowed to play with them. According to Amanda, "Mommy says 'You can't be too careful.' "

When questioned about school, Amanda squirmed in her chair. Finally, she reported that she liked her teacher, but the other children made fun of her clothes and her hair. She also reported that no one liked her because she threw up on the school bus. Amanda reported that she wanted a friend, but she didn't think she had one except for her Barbie.

Amanda reported that she had several cousins with whom she played at family get-togethers, but that they were all younger than she was. When questioned about her favorite television shows, Amanda reported that her parents didn't allow her to watch TV, but that she liked listening to Elvis Presley. When questioned about more recent music, Amanda was unable to describe any.

Although the interview had gone fairly well up to this point, Amanda began to be more anxious. She twisted around in the chair, stood up, then sat down, and finally asked if she could go see her mommy. The therapist decided that it was time to include the parents in the interview. Though normally the therapist preferred to interview the parents without the child, in this case it was felt that more information might be gained by having Amanda in the room, for at least part of the interview.

Mr. and Mrs. Anderson joined the therapist and Amanda. Once again, Amanda climbed up into her mother's lap. Although this may have been comfortable for a smaller child, Amanda's size made her attempts to sit in her mother's lap very awkward, especially since Mrs. Anderson was a relatively petite woman. Mr. Anderson attempted to get Amanda to sit next to him, but to no avail.

When questioned about the reason for the visit, Mrs. Anderson once again said to ask her husband because he was the one who saw a problem. Mr. Anderson, a soft-spoken but large man, leaned forward to express his concerns. He explained that he was concerned about Amanda because she was having difficulty making friends at school, hated going to school, and was frequently sick before school or on the school bus. He went on to state that his wife was a wonderful mother, but he was concerned that maybe she was such a good mother that Amanda didn't want to be away from her.

Mrs. Anderson reluctantly agreed with her husband's observations but denied that these behaviors were problematic. She stated that all children were different and Amanda was just going to be more of a "homebody" than other children.

Mr. Anderson went on to explain that he was a police detective who frequently worked long hours. While he was sometimes able to spend time with Amanda, his hours were dependent on the cases that he was working. Mrs. Anderson worked as a secretary in a local business and was home every day at 5 P.M. When Amanda got off the bus, she went to her maternal grandparent's home until her mother was finished working.

Mrs. Anderson reported that she and Amanda spent their time at church-related activities, cooking, sewing, or listening to music. When the therapist commented that Amanda had mentioned that her favorite singer was Elvis, Mr. Anderson nodded and said, "We don't allow any of that modern music in the house."

After much discussion, it seemed that Amanda began having difficulties several weeks after they had moved to their new house. In their old neighborhood, Amanda had been too little to be allowed to play with other children. They had moved to their present neighborhood when Amanda was six. In their new house, children had come to the house asking Amanda to play. Even though the children appeared fairly nice, Mrs. Anderson disapproved of the way the children were allowed to play in the yards rather than in the houses, and the fact that the other girls Amanda's age were allowed to ride their bicycles in the street. In addition, the other girls were allowed to watch television and listen to music of which the Andersons did not approve, such as music by Raffi, the Beatles, and Michael Jackson.

The major difficulties occurred around school. Since the beginning of kindergarten, Amanda dreaded going to school. Frequently she would become sick the night before a school day, a few minutes before the bus came, or on the bus. Even if Amanda did get to school, she frequently cried until the teachers, out of frustration, sent her home. In kindergarten, Amanda was sent home two to three times a week. In first grade, Amanda had only been sent home twice since the beginning of the year. Despite these problems, Amanda appeared to be performing well academically, earning all Bs on her first report card.

Mrs. Anderson reported that Amanda had no difficulty going to parties or sleepovers with her church friends or her relatives. Mr. Anderson, however, described one incident in which a neighborhood child had invited Amanda to a birthday party sleepover, and Amanda had come home after fifteen minutes. Amanda quietly stated that she was scared one of the girls might make fun of her.

Possible Diagnosis and Treatment Options

CASE 9 *Ian*

Ian was a small, eight-year-old boy enrolled in the third grade. His teacher, Mrs. Scott, has referred Ian to the school psychologist. Mrs. Scott reports that Ian has never spoken in her class despite the fact that school has been in session for two months. Although he completes all of his assignments, Ian refuses to interact with other children in the classroom or on the playground. In addition, Ian refuses to eat in the lunchroom. Mrs. Scott reports that Ian will whisper to a friend of his, Chris.

When interviewed by the school psychologist, Ian sat quietly in his chair. He did not fidget or move any body part throughout the interview. Physically, Ian is thin and shorter than the average third-grade boy. His blond hair is neatly cut and his jeans and shirt are neat and new-looking. There are no evident bruises or injuries.

Despite several attempts to engage Ian, he makes no response to the interviewer. Ian refuses to answer direct questions, refuses to play with toys, and refuses to draw or color. When told the interview was over, Ian jumps to his feet and quickly leaves the room.

The school psychologist then scheduled a meeting with Ian's parents. His parents arrived for the interview early and in separate cars. Ian's father explained that they had come from work, necessitating separate cars. Ian's father is a manager of a large grocery store. Ian's mother is employed as a computer consultant for a large corporation. Both parents are highly verbal and cooperative.

Ian was described by his parents as a shy child with few friends. Typically Ian makes one or two close friends in his class. Chris is his best friend in the third grade.

Ian is the youngest of two children. His sister, Kathy, is in the fifth grade and has no reported problems. Ian's mother reported no problems during her pregnancy or during labor and delivery. Developmental milestones were achieved within the normal age range. Talking was not a problem for Ian as a toddler. In fact, Ian's father reported that his preschool teacher would frequently complain that he talked too much.

No problems, other than shyness, were noted with Ian until he entered third grade. While Ian continued to receive high grades (all As), Mrs. Scott would send weekly notes reporting that Ian refused to talk, eat lunch, or interact with any child but Chris. Both of his parents tried discussing the problem with Ian, but he refused to give any reason for his change in behavior. Ian's mother suggested that his behavior might be "just a stage."

With permission of Chris's parents, Chris and Ian were brought to the interview room together. With Chris, Ian played with toy figures, raced cars, and drew pictures of cars and trucks. Ian whispered to Chris on several occasions, allowing Chris to report his comments to the interviewer. Ian still refused to answer any questions concerning his refusal to talk in school or his refusal to eat. He allowed Chris to report that he liked the other children but didn't want them to ask him questions. Chris volunteered that Ian quit talking during the previous summer after returning from a camping trip. Ian refused to answer any questions about the trip.

Possible Diagnosis and Treatment Options

CASE 10   *Chelsea*

Chelsea was first encountered by the therapist when she and her girlfriend came to a rape crisis center where the therapist was volunteering. The two high school girls had attended a party at a fraternity house the night before. During the evening the girls had become separated and Chelsea had returned to her home assuming her friend had already left. Unfortunately, her friend had passed out after consuming too many beers and had been raped while she was unconscious. The girls refused to report the incident to the police because they did not wish their parents to discover where they had been or that they had been drinking. Both of the girls were willing to allow the therapist to take them to a local hospital where Chelsea's friend could be treated.

The therapist remained with Chelsea while her friend was being seen by the physician. Chelsea was a petite, 5-foot, 2-inch, fifteen-year-old sophomore at the local high school. Her long black hair was held back in a ponytail and she wore tattered jeans, boots, and a flannel shirt. Her face was quite pale, emphasized by her black eyeliner, mascara, and stark red lipstick.

Chelsea appeared anxious about her friend and mumbled under her breath "it's my fault" repeatedly. The therapist tried to engage Chelsea in conversation, but the girl ignored her. After driving the girls back to the crisis center, the therapist handed the girls her card and told them to call anytime if they needed additional help.

Three months later, the therapist received a call from the campus police at 3 A.M. on a Sunday morning. The police officers had found a girl staggering down the road near some fraternity houses obviously drunk. The girl was unable to communicate clearly and had no identification on her. However, they had found the therapist's card in the pocket of her jeans. Assuming she must be a patient, they were holding the girl at the station while they contacted the therapist.

The therapist was surprised when she entered the station twenty minutes later to discover that the girl was Chelsea. By this point in time, the therapist had forgotten that she had given the two girls her cards. Chelsea was admitted to a local hospital because of the high alcohol content of her blood— 0.20.

The following morning the therapist was at the hospital when Chelsea awoke. At first, Chelsea was quite confused about her whereabouts and why the therapist was there. Once these questions were answered, she began crying. At first she was reluctant to give the therapist her last name or her telephone number because she was afraid of her parents' reactions. After some reassurance, Chelsea admitted her last name was Stanley and gave the therapist her telephone number. The therapist called Chelsea's parents from the phone next to Chelsea's bed. The Stanleys answered on the first ring and were relieved that their daughter was alive and well. The therapist explained the situation and, although upset about their daughter's alcohol use, they were anxious to get to the hospital. The therapist allowed Chelsea to speak to her parents and Chelsea began crying as her parents told her they loved her and were on their way to help her. When Chelsea hung up, she turned to the therapist with tears in her eyes and reported, amazed, that her parents didn't yell at her.

While waiting for her parents, Chelsea told the therapist that she had been drinking for three years. She began at school parties with beer. At first, the beer didn't taste very good and she didn't understand why all the kids drank. However, she wanted the other kids to like her and, with time, she found that she was more relaxed when she was drinking.

At additional parties, she had gravitated toward the vodka-spiked punch because it tasted better to her than the beer. She was able to drink much more of the punch and sometimes vomited before going home. By the end of her freshmen year in high school, she had discovered the parties on campus at the fraternity houses. She reported that she and her friends could go to these parties and drink all they wanted. Frequently, the guys at the fraternity would let the girls have a couple of bottles to take home with them so they could drink during the week. She and her friends would pour the bottles into water containers they would keep in their lockers at school. They could even take the water containers into class and the teachers never seemed to notice they were drinking alcohol.

Chelsea reported that the night her friend had been raped at the fraternity house was a blur to her. She remembered going to the party and drinking with some of the guys. The next thing she remembered was waking up in her bed with all of her clothes on. Chelsea cried as she reported that maybe if she hadn't been drunk her friend wouldn't have been raped. At that point, she had tried to quit drinking. She had managed not to drink on the Saturday or Sunday after the rape. On Monday, however, she attended school and the other girls were drinking, so she drank, too. Each day she would wake up and try not to drink but she always did.

When questioned about what made her drink each day, Chelsea was somewhat unsure but talked about her other friends who drank, the headaches when she awoke, and increasing anxiety until she took the first drink of the day. Chelsea reported that the night her friend was raped was the only night she had experienced any memory loss.

The Stanleys burst into the room at this point and immediately hugged their daughter. Mrs. Stanley was a small, plump woman in her early fifties. Her face was lined with worry about her daughter. She was dressed casually in black stretch pants and an oversized university sweatshirt. Mr. Stanley was a huge man, approximately 6 feet tall and weighing 300 pounds. He practically lifted his daughter off the bed as he hugged her.

Once they had reassured themselves that their daughter was alive and well, they seated themselves next to her bed and turned to the therapist. With Chelsea filling in the gaps, the therapist explained the information Chelsea had revealed concerning her alcohol abuse and her fear of telling her parents. Mrs. Stanley cried throughout the conversation while Mr. Stanley's face became grim.

Chelsea admitted to her parents that she had skipped school three times since the beginning of the year. She reported that she and her friends frequently snuck out early on Fridays so they could begin partying. Chelsea also started to hide her report cards as she was concerned that her parents would discover her truancy along with reports of missed exams.

Once the story was completed, Mr. Stanley turned to Chelsea and said in a firm voice, "Chelsea, my mother died from alcoholism and there is no way I'm going to let this get you too. We are all going to fight this together." He then asked the therapist if she could tell them what needed to be done to help Chelsea.

Possible Diagnosis and Possible Treatment Options

CASE 11 *Lee*

Lee Stratton was brought to the school psychologist's office around 2 P.M. on a Wednesday afternoon by a teacher, Mr. Burton. Mr. Burton's red face revealed his emerging anger. He carried a shoebox filled with Baggies, which he slammed onto the psychologist's desk before seating himself and motioning for Lee to sit. The psychologist noted that Lee seemed to be having some difficulty walking in a straight line from the door to his chair and almost missed the seat as he dropped into the chair. Mr. Burton reported that he had heard noises in the men's restroom and had gone to investigate. Upon entering, he had found Lee vomiting in one of the stalls. At first he had been concerned that Lee was ill. Upon helping Lee stand and clean himself, Mr. Burton had observed that Lee's speech was slurred, he was staggering, and he reeked of alcohol and marijuana. The teacher concluded that Lee was drunk. At this point, Mr. Burton had become enraged and ordered Lee to open his locker. Lee had obeyed, whereupon Mr. Burton had found the shoebox. Mr. Burton leaned across the psychologist's desk and dumped the box scattering three plastic bags, several bottles of Nyquil, and a water container. Two of the plastic bags contained loose marijuana and the third contained joints. Mr. Burton unscrewed the lid of the water container saying, "See?" as the smell of alcohol permeated the room.

Once Mr. Burton had been sent to talk with the headmaster, the psychologist faced Lee. Lee was a white, twelve-year-old seventh grader with curly brown hair, brown eyes, and a muscular build. Currently, Lee's shirt had splotches of water on it, his eyes were reddened, and his face was pale.

The psychologist first phoned Lee's parents. Mr. Stratton was at work, but Mrs. Stratton was at home and agreed to come to the school immediately. While they waited for Lee's mother, the psychologist talked with Lee.

At first, Lee answered in a quiet, frightened tone of voice with definite slurring of speech. He admitted that he had been drinking since he got to school that morning and had smoked a joint at lunch. He denied that any of his friends were involved. As Lee talked, color returned to his face and he became more relaxed. As he relaxed, he also became sarcastic. First Lee complained about the teacher forcing him to open his locker, stating that his Dad was an attorney and that the drugs couldn't be used against him because it was an illegal search. He then taunted the psychologist by claiming that his parents paid "a lot of money" for him to attend the school and that "no way" the school would be willing to lose that money by making trouble for him. Finally Lee asked the psychologist what his "problem" was, since "everyone smoked pot," and that his parents smoked with him almost every weekend. Lee also reported that this wasn't the first time he had drunk at school. He reported that he brought alcohol to school two to three times a week and Mr. Burton was the only one who seemed upset.

At this point, Mrs. Stratton arrived at the office with the headmaster. Once both of them had been seated, the psychologist explained what Mr. Burton and Lee had reported. Mrs. Stratton's face turned white as she listened to the psychologist. Once the psychologist had finished, the headmaster stood and stated that his hands were tied. Lee would be suspended three days and would be allowed to return to school only as long as he submitted to daily locker searches and saw the school psychologist once a week. Mrs. Stratton weakly agreed and the headmaster returned to his own office.

In the ensuing quietness following the headmaster's departure, the psychologist studied Mrs. Stratton. Her coloring matched that of her son, although she was petite in contrast to his muscular build. She was dressed in designer sweats and wore a diamond tennis bracelet. Since entering the room, she had made no effort to touch or comfort her son.

Lee glanced at the psychologist before talking to his mother. He laughed awkwardly and told her not to worry, three days of vacation would let him catch up on his homework and his sleep. Mrs. Stratton turned and stared at her son. Finally, a visible shudder went through her before she answered.

"Shut up!" she hissed through clenched teeth. She turned to the psychologist and asked if she could take her son home. The psychologist granted permission but requested that she, her husband, and her son return to the office the next morning. He asked how the Strattons were planning to punish Lee.

Appearing confused, Mrs. Stratton agreed to the meeting and reported that Lee would be confined to his room. When asked if Lee had a computer, TV, or stereo in his room, Mrs. Stratton reported that he did. The psychologist suggested that these items be removed, leaving Lee with his bed, his clothing, and his school books. Mrs. Stratton seemed worried about this but agreed to follow the psychologist's instructions until they could meet the next day.

The following day Lee and his parents arrived at the psychologist's office at the appointed time. Lee was clean and dressed in khaki dress pants, an oxford shirt, and a navy blazer. His mother was also dressed more formally in a dress and heels. Mr. Stratton was dressed identically to his son.

After being seated, Mr. Stratton began the conversation by inquiring whether the school had informed the authorities about the contents of Lee's locker. The psychologist told the Strattons that the school's policy was not to inform the authorities on a student's first offense. Although this policy may not have been strictly legal, the school wished to give each student an opportunity to correct his or her behavior. The Strattons appeared to relax as the psychologist explained the school's policy.

Mr. Stratton answered most of the questions unless they were specifically addressed to Lee or Mrs. Stratton. According to the Strattons, they believed that children should be allowed to use alcohol in moderation but were not aware of Lee's alcohol use at school nor his marijuana use. Mr. Stratton denied that he or his wife smoked marijuana.

After much discussion, Lee and his parents agreed that Lee would meet with the psychologist once a week after school and that his parents would join him once a month. Lee also agreed to submit to daily locker searches as dictated by the school.

Possible Diagnosis and Treatment Options

CASE 12   *Cathy*

When first interviewed by the examiner, Cathy was lying in a hospital bed on the psychiatric ward of a local hospital. She had been admitted the previous afternoon for attempting to kill herself in the school restroom. A fellow student had discovered Cathy in the restroom during afternoon classes. Cathy had slashed her wrists with a kitchen knife she had apparently brought to school from her home. The clinician was asked to interview Cathy to determine why she was suicidal and to provide a diagnosis.

Cathy, a fourteen-year-old, white female with shoulder-length blonde hair, large brown eyes, and pale skin, was small for her age, weighing 90 pounds and standing 5 feet tall. Upon entering the room, the clinician observed Cathy lying on the bed. She had pulled the sheet up to her nose so that only the top half of her head could be seen.

Cathy spoke in a whisper throughout the initial interview. Although she attempted to answer all of the examiner's questions, her answers were frequently illogical and rambling. Cathy reported that she was in the eighth grade and enjoyed art class but did not like any other classes. She also reported that she did not have any friends at school because all of the kids were "stupid." Cathy explained that the kids were not always so stupid but that, "after the invaders took over the school," she lost all of her friends. When questioned, Cathy indicated that the invasion took place the previous summer, but that the troops were still trying to take over the town. Cathy then indicated the noise of the helicopters outside the hospital window was evidence of the troops. While the hospital did have an emergency helicopter, the examiner had not heard any helicopter land or depart during the interview. Upon further questioning, Cathy indicated that she was afraid the troops would learn that she had not become stupid like the other kids. She stated that once this was discovered, the troops would take her to their camp, remove her brain, and replace it with a washing machine. Cathy denied hearing voices, but reported that she was very religious and believed that God talked with her on a daily basis. She stated that she was grateful for these conversations with God; otherwise she believed she would have "gone crazy."

Cathy reported no changes in her sleeping or eating behavior and ap-

parently sleeps seven to eight hours a night. She indicated that she had difficulty concentrating on her schoolwork because she was afraid she would be
discovered by the troops. When directly questioned about her suicide attempt, Cathy reported that she didn't really want to die, but that death was
preferable to being captured by the troops. She seemed very puzzled that her
suicide attempt was discovered, for she had chosen the school restroom over
her home as a "more private place."

Given the seriousness of the situation, the lack of coherent answers, and
the numerous questions not answered by Cathy, her parents were interviewed by the examiner. Cathy's parents arrived for the scheduled interview
accompanied by their two other children. Cathy's mother stated that she just
didn't trust babysitters and that she was sure the children would be no problem. Cathy's mother was approximately forty years of age with graying black
hair that was shabbily cut but clean. Likewise, her clothing was shabby but
clean. Cathy's father was approximately the same age as Cathy's mother. He
was dressed in army fatigues, army boots, and his hair was cut in a crew-cut.
Shelly, their thirteen-year-old daughter, wore designer jeans, expensive tennis shoes and jewelry, and a polo shirt. Aaron, their four-year-old son, was
dressed in a patched pair of jeans and a ripped t-shirt. Interestingly, his
clothes and face were quite dirty.

Cathy's father began the interview by stating that he was very angry
that the hospital would not release Cathy. He explained that he was sure the
suicide attempt was just a misunderstanding and that the best thing for Cathy
would be a "good swat on the butt." He stated that coddling Cathy would
just lead to more "attention-seeking." He explained that ever since Cathy was
a baby she had "acted up in one way or another," in an effort to get more attention. He believed that Cathy was jealous of her sister Shelly, who was very
popular, a natural athlete, a good student, and "just darned cute."

When asked about Cathy's early years, Cathy's father began tapping his
foot and staring at the ceiling. Cathy's mother then answered all questions in
a tremulous voice. She reported that Cathy was a sickly baby who had frequent ear infections and spit up most of her food. She walked at about fifteen
months of age, but didn't begin to talk until she was almost three. Although
Shelly was a year younger than Cathy, it was Shelly who seemed to be the big-
ger sister as she talked before Cathy, and had many more friends than Cathy.
Cathy's mother reported that Cathy preferred to spend her time daydreaming
and drawing in her sketchbook. While Cathy's grades in school were quite
variable (one time earning a D in a subject and the next time earning an A in
the same subject), this was the first time Cathy had been in any "serious
trouble."

According to her mother, Cathy had been spending more and more time
alone in recent months. Prior to this time, Cathy had one friend with whom
she would go to movies and art shows at the museum. Cathy's mother was
fairly sure the friendship had ended the previous summer though she was

unaware of the reason. Over the past eight months, Cathy has become more and more upset about her father's guns and military clothing. She even claimed that her father was one of the "troops" and that God didn't approve of his fighting. Cathy's mother stated that she just ignored her daughter's complaints because Cathy didn't really make much sense and there were two other children who needed attention.

Cathy's mother described herself as a full-time homemaker and stated that her husband was a car salesman. When questioned about the fatigues, Cathy's father reported that he was part of a militia group that trained for imminent war with the government. He stated that he had plans for a training session in South America the coming weekend. At this point, Shelly entered the conversation, saying that she wished she could accompany her father so that she could have fun, too. Cathy's father hugged his daughter and reassured her that she could accompany him when she was sixteen. While Cathy's father hugged Shelly, Aaron climbed into his mother's lap and started to pull at her blouse. Cathy's mother looked at the therapist and asked if the interview was over because she needed to breastfeed the baby.

Possible Diagnosis and Treatment Options

CASE 13 *Anne*

Anne Gillespie was brought to the community mental health center by her mother, Ms. Newsome. The therapist assigned to the case first met with Ms. Newsome while Anne waited. Ms. Newsome was dressed in a navy blue business suit with a white blouse and high heels. Her hair was brown, tinged with gray, styled simply but carefully in a chignon. Other than gold earrings, Ms. Newsome wore no other jewelry.

When asked why she had wanted her daughter to see a therapist, Ms. Newsome carefully explained that she wasn't a religious person. Although she and her daughter were Christians and celebrated Christmas, Easter, and so on, they didn't attend church and her daughter had not even been baptized. The therapist was confused by this outpouring and asked Ms. Newsome if she felt her daughter needed to be baptized. Ms. Newsome giggled nervously, and stated that she hoped it wouldn't be too late to baptize her daughter because she was concerned that Anne might be a Satanist.

Ms. Newsome reported that she and Anne lived alone in a house she had purchased after her divorce four years ago. Her ex-husband currently lived in another state with his present wife. By her own choice, Anne had no contact with her father. The divorce had been an amicable one after her ex-husband impregnated his secretary. Ms. Newsome reported that she had never minded his affairs, but that getting his secretary pregnant was "too much." She reported that Anne did not seem unduly upset with the divorce, and she continued to attend the same school with her friends. The major change for Anne was a new house which Anne had been pleased with because it had an in-ground pool. The divorce was not a problem financially, as Ms. Newsome was a bank vice-president and made sufficient money of her own.

Over the past year, Ms. Newsome had noticed a change in her daughter. Anne had dropped her old friends and now spent most of her time in her room. She rarely had friends over to the house, and those who had been to the house were different than her previous friends. In addition, her grades had dropped from As and Bs to mainly Cs. Finally, she had dyed her blond hair black and cut one side short while leaving the other side long. Ms. Newsome had been concerned but not alarmed by these events; she remembered her own teenage years during the late 1960s, when "everyone" wore their hair long, smoked pot, and wore "love beads."

The previous night, Ms. Newsome had awakened in the middle of the night to hear chanting coming from her daughter's room. As she walked down the hall, she smelled an odd scent. Upon opening her daughter's door, she saw her daughter standing in the middle of her room, naked, surrounded by flickering candles with her upraised arms clutching a knife dripping with blood. Ms. Newsome had screamed and run back to her room.

By the time she had calmed herself and went back to Anne's room, Anne was dressed in pajamas and was washing the bloody knife in her bathroom sink. When questioned, Anne had irritably replied that her mother should respect her privacy and not barge into her room. Anne could not be cajoled into telling her mother anything about her actions.

Ms. Newsome told the therapist that she was concerned that her daughter was part of some cult, and that they had killed an animal or even a baby. She went on to report that she had read books about cults but had never considered that such a thing went on in her own town, much less her own home.

Anne was brought into the therapist's office while Ms. Newsome was asked to wait in a separate room. Anne was of average height but weighed significantly less than average. She was dressed in loose black jeans, a long-sleeved black shirt, and black boots. Her hair had been dyed black, poorly, and just as her mother had described, one side was long and straight while the other was cut in short spikes. Anne's face had been dusted with a white powder and her eyes outlined in black. Her movements were jerky and perceptibly slower than expected. Rather than a fourteen-year-old white teenager, Anne looked the part of a character in a vampire or zombie movie.

Anne sat in the chair indicated by the therapist without speaking. When asked why she thought she was in the center, Anne replied in a monotone that her mother had "freaked out." She went on to explain, after considerable prompting, that her mother had come into her room unannounced and discovered her while she was praying. Anne's speech was coherent but slow and monotone in quality. When asked to describe how she prayed, Anne described how she had come to know the power of Satan and that she felt relief when praying to him. The prayers consisted of standing naked in the center of a circle of lighted candles while cutting herself with a ceremonial knife. Satan required the blood to take away her anxieties and problems.

When questioned about her problems, Anne became vague, but commented that she found it difficult to get to sleep at night, frequently staying awake until 2 or 3 A.M., worrying about the mistakes she had made at school and her parents' divorce. Once at school, she found it hard to concentrate on what the teachers said, and spent most of her time staring out of the windows. Upon more detailed questioning by the therapist, Anne admitted that her problems had been gradually increasing since the divorce but had become worse over the past year. In the past year, Anne reported that she had lost

15 pounds without any attempt at dieting and is always irritable. Anne also reported that she believes she was at least partially responsible for her parents' divorce, as she was a "real brat" for a year before the divorce. She reported that she frequently thought that her parents might get back together if she was dead. Anne denied suicidal intent or plan. She described the self-cutting as part of her prayers and described how they lifted her spirits for a few seconds.

When questioned about her friends, Anne reported that her new friends were the ones who had introduced her to worshiping Satan. She denied any cult involvement, reporting that the other girls had lent her several books and had shown her the various chants. Anne also denied drug use. She reported that she had tried smoking cigarettes but did not like the smell. Although she had been offered pot, she had no interest in it. Alcohol had always been present in her house, but Anne reported that she had no desire to drink.

When asked what she enjoyed, Anne grimaced slightly as she reported that she used to enjoy everything—going shopping with her friends, swimming, riding her bike—but that now everything seemed to take too much energy. She reported that she spent most of her time in her room listening to music or reading her book about Satan. She noted that even that wasn't "fun" but simply passed the time.

Possible Diagnosis and Treatment Options

CASE 14   *Jacob*

Seven-year-old Jacob Samuels was referred to the school psychologist by his second-grade teacher after the first parent-teacher conference. Despite setting an appointment to meet with Jacob's parents, no parent had attended.

According to Mrs. Lonetto, Jacob had spent the first two months of school sitting at his desk. Jacob did not stand for the pledge of allegiance, he did not walk around the room, and he did not go to the chalkboard when asked. Jacob followed the children to the cafeteria for lunch but rarely ate more than one or two bites. Jacob consistently sat by himself in the cafeteria and rarely acknowledged the other children even when they began conversations with him. Despite this "shyness," Jacob usually completed his schoolwork in a satisfactory manner and would answer direct questions from the teacher. Mrs. Lonetto expressed concern that she believed Jacob was more than shy, but that she was uncomfortable referring him to the psychologist before discussing the issue with Jacob's parents.

The Samuels agreed to meet with the psychologist the following week. Unfortunately, they did not keep the appointment. At this point, the principal was recruited and called the parents. Once again an appointment was scheduled. This time, the Samuels arrived for the appointment ten minutes early.

Mr. Samuels worked for his father's plumbing supply business. He was a short man in his early thirties with dark hair and beard dressed in clean khakis and an oxford shirt. Mrs. Samuels was not employed. She cared for the couple's three children. Jacob, at seven, was the oldest. Jennifer, aged five, and Jordan, aged three, were being watched by their paternal grandmother while the Samuels met with the psychologist.

Mrs. Samuels, a small woman in her late twenties with long dark hair and nervous habits, explained that she had been unable to make the previous two meetings due to her younger children. She stated that she didn't believe in children being left with babysitters and that she needed to get home as soon as possible.

The Samuels were surprised to learn that Jacob had been referred to the school psychologist. Mr. Samuels reported that Jacob was a good child who rarely had to be disciplined. Mrs. Samuels concurred, stating that Jacob had always been an easy baby who picked up his own toys and kept his room fairly clean. The Samuels reported that Jacob had achieved his developmental milestones within normal range—walking at twelve months, potty-trained at three years. Jacob had begun reading on his own the summer before he began kindergarten. Jacob had not attended daycare or preschool. The Samuels knew of no problems Jacob might have had in adjusting to kindergarten or first grade. When questioned about friends, Mrs. Samuels reported that Jacob much preferred reading or playing with his sisters to playing with other children.

The following day, Jacob was brought to the psychologist's office. Jacob was a small child with straight dark hair and large brown eyes. He was dressed neatly in blue pants and striped shirt. While he glanced around the office, he never made eye contact with the psychologist. Jacob sat in the chair indicated by the psychologist but failed to play with any of the toys sitting on the desk or floor even after being encouraged.

Jacob reported that he was the oldest of three children, but that he wished he was the youngest because Jordan didn't have any chores. When questioned about his chores, Jacob stated that he had to make his bed each morning, change his sheets once a week, take out the garbage every night, and feed and water the dog. He reported that his chores weren't hard but they interfered with his reading.

Jacob reported that school was "okay" although he couldn't think of anything that he liked or disliked about school. When asked about his friends in his class, Jacob reported that he didn't have any friends at school. When questioned, Jacob stated that he didn't mind not having friends at school because it was better not to get into trouble anyway.

When questioned about his favorite activities, Jacob reported that he used to love reading but that he didn't feel like reading much anymore. Jacob reported that since school began, he had been having trouble sleeping and frequently would not fall asleep until midnight. After being awake so late, Jacob reported that it was more and more difficult for him to get out of bed the next morning and go to school. After much probing, Jacob revealed that he couldn't sleep because he was worrying about things he had done. He reported that he didn't want his mom to know how "bad" he had been. Jacob reported that he sometimes thought about pushing his brother, Jordan, off the swing or not doing his chores. His eyes watered as he explained that his mother loved them very much and he was always thinking mean things about her in his head—how she was too bossy and wouldn't let him alone.

Based on the interview, Jacob and the psychologist completed the Children's Depression Inventory together. The CDI was created from the Beck Depression Inventory designed for adults. With the CDI, the child chooses one of three responses to twenty-seven items reflecting behavioral, affective, and cognitive dimensions of depression. The child responds according to which alternative best characterizes them over the past two-week period.

On the basis of the CDI, Jacob scored in the moderately depressed category with his highest scores in sleeping problems, eating problems, loss of pleasure in everyday activities, social isolation, and feeling sad. Suicidal ideation was reported but no suicidal intent or gestures were noted.

Possible Diagnosis and Treatment Options

CASE 15   *Carly*

Mr. and Mrs. Prochaski were referred to the therapist by their daughter's school counselor, Lisa Hammett. Carly, aged fifteen, was a sophomore at the local high school. Prior to the last grading period Carly had consistently earned As in her courses, even though she was enrolled in honors courses. Ms. Hammett had contacted the Prochaskis when Carly's teachers had indicated that Carly was failing all of her courses. Although Ms. Hammett had initially spoken with Carly, she did not believe that Carly was responsive to her concerns.

The Prochaskis and Carly arrived for their appointment on time. Carly was interviewed by the therapist first. Carly was a slim fifteen-year-old of clear Native American ancestry. She wore jeans, a t-shirt, and boots. Carly described her problem as one of her "parents overreacting." She acknowledged that her grades had dropped but reported that she knew the material. Carly reported that science was her favorite subject, especially when they studied astronomy. She stated that she disliked history. When asked, Carly reported that she slept fine and had no concerns other than she had gained 10 pounds in the past month. She denied feelings of sadness although she did report a loss of interest in usual activities such as attending movies with her friends and soccer. When questioned about friends, Carly reported that she had plenty of friends. She stated that her best friend was Diane who played on the same soccer team and with whom she frequently went to the mall. She could not remember the last time they had gone to the mall but thought it might have been about two months ago. Carly denied drug use but acknowledged she had tried beer at a party. However, she stated she had decided not to start drinking because she had heard that as a Native American she had more of a chance of becoming an alcoholic. When questioned, Carly reported that she had been given up for adoption and knew nothing of her biological parents other than that they were Native American and still in high school when her mother became pregnant. Carly reported that she wished her biological parents had kept her as she frequently felt out of place among Caucasians.

The Prochaskis were interviewed after Carly. Mr. Prochaski was in his late fifties and dressed in a business suit. He worked as a representative for a college textbook publisher. Mrs. Prochaski was also in her late fifties but was dressed more casually in a print dress. Both of the Prochaskis were blond and blue-eyed. The Prochaskis reported that they had adopted Carly when she was three days old. They confirmed Carly's report that she was born to Native American biological parents. Their understanding was that her biological parents were still in high school and simply too young and too poor to care for a baby. They had also been informed that the biological mother did not drink alcohol during her pregnancy. Mrs. Prochaski stated that she had been concerned about this as "Indians are known to have trouble with alcohol."

Mrs. Prochaski reported that she was unable to have children and that Carly was the perfect baby. She noted that Carly had attained her developmental milestones at the appropriate ages and had always been extremely healthy. Carly had earned As in every subject since first grade and was the star of her soccer team. Mrs. Prochaski reported that she was confused as to why Carly's grades were so bad. She asked the interviewer if Carly could be mad at her for getting a job. Prior to this year, Mrs. Prochaski had stayed home full-time. This fall, she had obtained a job as a receptionist for a physician.

The Prochaskis reported that they had not noticed any changes in Carly's behavior. She slept well, frequently having to be aroused in order to avoid being late for school. Mr. Prochaski noted that Carly had finally put on a little weight, which he was pleased to see, as she had always been too thin. Both Prochaskis reported that Carly seemed well-liked by her peers but was not spending much time with them lately. They described Carly as spending most of her free time in her room, studying, or practicing soccer. Mrs. Prochaski noted that she was glad Carly was devoting herself to her studies and not spending as much time at the mall with her friends.

The interviewer asked the Prochaskis if Carly had expressed any interest in her Native American heritage or any concerns about not "fitting in." The Prochaskis reported that adoption officials had been somewhat concerned about this issue too, so the Prochaskis had made a point of providing Carly with books about Native Americans and made sure that she always got to play the part of the "Indian" in any school plays. They recalled that in 5th grade she was able to play the part of Pocahontas in the class play. They stated that they had not taken Carly to any reservations because they did not want her to see "how lazy those people were."

Carly was brought back into the room to join her parents for the final part of the interview. The interviewer reported that Carly's low grades were of concern and that several issues needed to be explored further. Permission, and written consent, was obtained to interview Carly's school counselor and her teachers. In addition, Carly was scheduled for psychological tests for the following week.

On the following day, the interviewer met with Carly's school counselor, Lisa Hammett. Ms. Hammett was clearly relieved to meet with the interviewer, stating that she had been happy to cancel another appointment to make time for the meeting. She reported that she was very concerned about Carly. In the past Carly had been one of the school's brightest stars. Carly was brilliant, athletic, friendly, and gracious. She excelled in the classroom as well as on the soccer field. Over the past nine weeks, Ms. Hammett had noticed disturbing changes in Carly. In addition to her falling grades, due solely to a failure to turn in any homework despite the homework being in her folders, Carly had missed half of the soccer practices including an important game. Prior to this time Carly had never missed a soccer practice or game, even when she was ill. Even more disturbing was the change in how she interacted with others. Whereas she had always smiled and greeted others in a friendly way, she now walked the halls "in a daze" not even greeting her friends. Finally, Ms. Hammett reported that she felt she had to contact the Prochaskis when Carly's English teacher had brought her a poem Carly had written. Carly described the world as a wintry place, without love or warmth. At the end of the poem, the speaker lies down in the snow awaiting death. Ms. Hammett's concern was that Carly was describing her own feelings and was contemplating suicide.

On the morning of the scheduled assessment appointment with Carly, the interviewer received a call from Carly's mother. The previous night Carly had taken a bottle of aspirin. When her parents could not awaken her for dinner, they discovered the empty bottle and had taken her to the hospital. She was currently in the hospital, in fair condition. According to Mrs. Prochaski the physicians had indicated that Carly had not taken enough aspirin to kill herself. The hospital psychologist had agreed to work with the interviewer and suggested that Mrs. Prochaski call.

Possible Diagnosis and Treatment Options

CASE 16   *Michael*

Michael Sundersen was referred to the school psychologist by his second-grade teacher, Ms. Russell. Michael had been playing on the playground during recess when six other boys had begun teasing him, tripping him, and eventually kicking and hitting him. Michael did not fight back but sat on the ground and cried. According to Ms. Russell, Michael appeared more effeminate than the other boys and chose to play with the girls on the playground. On more than one occasion Michael had announced to the teacher or a playmate that he would be a girl when he was an adult. While most of the children were fairly tolerant of Michael, Ms. Russell reported that she had noticed increased teasing and shunning of Michael by the other children.

Michael came into the office cautiously. Michael was small for an eight-year old, with delicate bones and blond hair touching his shoulders. He wore clean blue jeans and an oxford shirt. When Michael sat, he pressed both legs tightly together and crossed them at the ankle. When addressed by the therapist, Michael was quite cooperative, speaking in a soft, almost feminine tone of voice punctuated by giggles.

According to Michael, he lived with his mother and older sister, Anna, who was ten. Michael reported that his parents had divorced when Michael was three and he had not seen his father since. Michael went on to report that he enjoyed schoolwork, especially reading and spelling. He did not like the other boys but enjoyed playing with the girls. At home, he mainly played Barbies with his sister. He reported that he enjoyed watching television, with *Full House* being his favorite show. Michael also reported that he wanted to be a teacher or a nurse when he grew up. When questioned about more stereotypic "male" behaviors such as sports, Michael responded that he didn't like sports. When asked if he liked being a boy, Michael paused, then reported that he wasn't really a boy, that his mom just thought he was. When he grew up he would be a girl.

Mrs. Sundersen confirmed Michael's self-report stating that her ex-husband was from Sweden and had returned there after their divorce. Mrs. Sundersen worked as a nurse in a local hospital. When she wasn't home, the children were watched by her mother. She reported that Michael and Anna had always played well together with Anna dressing her baby brother in doll clothes until he was four. Mrs. Sundersen reported that she had some "cute" pictures of Michael dressed in a dress with high heels and makeup. When asked about the length of Michael's hair, Mrs. Sundersen stated that she didn't want to cut his beautiful hair and planned to put it in a pony tail when he got older. Mrs. Sundersen also confirmed Michael's report that he believed he would be a girl when he grew up. She stated that Michael had been saying that "for years" and she had given up trying to convince him otherwise. She reported that her physician had even tried to talk with Michael but to no avail. She went on to ask, "Wouldn't he be a beautiful girl?"

Possible Diagnosis and Treatment Options

CASE 17 *Elizabeth*

Elizabeth Fellows was referred to the therapist by her physician. Elizabeth, a fifteen-year-old Caucasian, was taken to her physician by her mother after her mother overheard her vomiting in the bathroom. The physician had referred her to the therapist after ascertaining that there was no physical cause for her vomiting. A medical report accompanied the referral outlining the physician's concerns about a possible eating disorder.

Elizabeth and her mother came to the first session together. Mrs. Fellows was dressed in a pleated skirt and white blouse. Though not obese, Mrs. Fellows was somewhat overweight. Elizabeth was dressed in tight jeans and an oversized sweatshirt. She also was overweight, although not as much as her mother.

Elizabeth's mother asked to be seen first. Once seated, Mrs. Fellows reported that she was worried about her daughter. Not only had she heard Elizabeth vomiting in the bathroom on three occasions, but Elizabeth had dropped all of her friends and stayed home in her bedroom. Mrs. Fellows went on to report that until approximately six months ago Elizabeth seemed fairly normal to her. Since that time Elizabeth has spent more and more time by herself, dropping even her best friend, Katie, with whom she had been friends since kindergarten. Previously, Elizabeth had been a straight-A student; now she was earning Bs and Cs. Mrs. Fellows acknowledged that Elizabeth's tenth grade year was a difficult one but that she felt Elizabeth's personality was changing. Mrs. Fellows was unable to remember any significant event that had occurred in the past six months that might explain her daughter's behavior.

Mrs. Fellows went on to report that she and Elizabeth's father were divorced when Elizabeth was two. Mrs. Fellows had married her current husband when Elizabeth was three. She went on to report that her current husband and Elizabeth got along very well. Elizabeth was their only child.

When Elizabeth entered the therapy room, she walked slowly and eased herself into a chair. While her clothing was clean, Elizabeth's hair was greasy and tied messily back into a pony tail. Lesions on her right hand were evident. While answering all questions, Elizabeth responded slowly and, at times, had to be prompted to answer.

Elizabeth reported that she was in the tenth grade at the local high school and, up to this year, had enjoyed school. She reported that she had been unable to concentrate on her studies this year, resulting in her grades falling. When questioned about why she had trouble concentrating, Elizabeth was vague, stating that she had "a lot" on her mind. After additional questioning, Elizabeth reported that she thinks about food most of the day. She reported that she plans each meal and her binges. While her parents eat, Elizabeth plans which of the leftovers she can eat without their knowledge. When questioned about her friends, Elizabeth reported that she didn't feel like doing things with her friends. She denied any fights with her friends, stating that she just didn't find anything enjoyable any more.

When questioned about the vomiting incidents, Elizabeth explained that she had learned this from her friends in the ninth grade. Elizabeth reported that she had been binge-eating and vomiting for about eight months. In the beginning, she only vomited at school along with her friends. After eating, they would all go to the bathroom and stick their fingers down their throat until they vomited. This way they could eat what they wanted and not gain any weight. Elizabeth sadly reported that she didn't lose as much weight as the others because she was binge-eating too much. During the summer, though, she had begun vomiting after each meal and had begun her binge-eating in the middle of the night. She reported that two or three times a week she would go to the kitchen after her parents were asleep and eat. During these "raids" she would consume whatever she could find. Last night, for example, she had eaten a half-gallon of ice cream and half of a chocolate cake. Afterwards, she had vomited in the bathroom. She reported that before a binge, she would become more and more excited, but that after binge-eating she would get "antsy" and feel disgusted with herself until she vomited. She felt ashamed of her behavior and had not told Katie or her other friends. She reported that she was embarrassed that her mother was making such a big deal of her vomiting, but that she was also relieved that she could talk about it with someone who would understand.

With further questioning, Elizabeth reported that she knew other girls who binged and vomited but that no one she knew did it as much as she did. She also reported that over the past three months she found herself more and more depressed about herself and her actions. She admitted that she had considered killing herself, but did not seriously think she would do it because she knew her parents would be so hurt.

Possible Diagnosis and Treatment Options

CASE 18 *Maria*

Maria, a twelve-year-old African American girl, was referred to the therapist for treatment by her physician. Approximately one year prior to referral, the client had been hospitalized for rheumatic fever, which resulted in permanent heart damage. Despite her strongly expressed desire to lose weight and her physician's efforts to help her diet, Maria had gained weight steadily over the past year, reporting to the therapist with a weight of 258 pounds. The physician reported no thyroid problems that might lead to Maria's problems with her weight.

Maria reported that she had been overweight since she was an infant. Her mother, who accompanied her to the initial session, was also obese, weighing in excess of 350 pounds. However, the remainder of the family (father, two sisters, and one brother) were of average or slightly below average weight.

At the initial session, Maria and her mother were interviewed. She and her mother were scheduled for weekly one-hour sessions. Maria was weighed at the beginning of each session. During the first session, self-monitoring was introduced and explained. In order to establish a baseline of her food intake, the client was asked to keep a daily record detailing (1) the type and quantity of food and drink consumed, (2) environmental cues related to eating, (3) eating style (degree of hunger and rate of eating), and (4) the emotional and cognitive aspects of eating. She was not asked to make any changes in her behavior during this baseline monitoring.

The same format was followed during the four subsequent sessions. Weigh-in was followed by a review of the client's progress during the previous week, based on the food records and self-reports. Maria was encouraged to devise problem-solving strategies to deal with any difficulties encountered, and nutrition and exercise information was presented during these four sessions. The nutritional component included information on the basic food groups; maintaining a balanced diet low in fat, sugar, and salt; specific methods of preparing food; and misconceptions about diet and nutrition. Maria, not her mother, was responsible for preparing and eating the appropriate foods. Increasing physical activity was encouraged and the caloric expense of exercise and methods for gradually increasing energy expenditure were discussed.

Despite these measures, Maria continued to gain weight during the course of treatment, going from an initial weight of 258 pounds to a weight of 265 pounds at the end of five weeks. She frequently left her self-monitoring sheets at home or returned them incomplete. In addition, her mother expressed frustration, reporting several instances in which her daughter had failed to record between-meal snacks she had eaten. Maria, however, denied that her records were inaccurate.

At this point the mother wanted to terminate treatment because she felt her daughter was not serious about losing weight. Both Maria and her mother agreed to continue treatment for another six weeks, but with the addition of the entire family.

The entire family participated at the next session. For the first time since the beginning of treatment, Maria's weight dropped at the weigh-in (from 265 to 264 pounds). However, once again, Maria did not return her self-monitoring sheets. The family was asked to report on the client's food consumption and several family members reported that the client ate ice cream, cake, and candy in the afternoons at her grandmother's house. Maria verified the accuracy of these reports for the first time. Those situations in which Maria had difficulty controlling her food intake were discussed, as were strategies for dealing with such situations in the future.

The family failed to attend the following session, and at weigh-in, Maria had gained two pounds. During this session, the importance of family involvement was emphasized. The following week, the family once again accompanied Maria, who, at weigh-in, had lost just over 3 pounds. Despite further emphasis on family involvement, Maria arrived the following week by herself, having gained approximately 1 pound.

After this session, Maria failed to keep her appointments. When contacted by the therapist a year and a half later, she had continued to gain weight, reporting her current weight at 310 pounds. A few weeks after this conversation, Maria's mother contacted the therapist with a plea to see her daughter in therapy again. Two days before, Maria had been readmitted to the hospital because of heart problems. Maria's physician had told the family that Maria would be dead before she was twenty-one if she didn't lose her excess weight. The therapist agreed to see Maria for an initial interview and assessment.

Possible Diagnosis and Treatment Options

CASE 19   *Lisa*

Lisa, a seventeen-year-old freshman at a large state university, was brought to the therapist over Christmas break. Lisa was approximately 5 feet, 8 inches and weighed 90 pounds. She was dressed in sweats with a university logo. Her hair was attractively styled and her makeup expertly applied.

During the first part of the interview, Lisa sat quietly between her parents allowing them to answer all questions. Mrs. Baker was an attractive woman in her forties. She was petite, thin, and her hair was dyed blond. She was dressed neatly in a conservative suit. Mr. Baker was also dressed in a suit. He was a tall, muscular man in his forties. Both were employed in sales.

Mrs. Baker reported that she and her husband have brought Lisa to see a therapist at the insistence of Lisa's dorm counselor. The counselor had called the parents because of her concern over Lisa's diminishing weight and unusual eating patterns. When she began college, Lisa weighed 115 pounds. Over the past 4 months, Lisa had lost 25 pounds. The dorm counselor reported that Lisa did not eat breakfast or lunch. At dinner she got a tray, cleaned the tray with a napkin, centered a plate on the tray, got a bowl, centered the bowl on the plate, and then centered her food in the bowl. Her food varied each evening. One evening Lisa might have selected five green beans. Another evening it might have been five pickle slices or five slices of apple. Once the food was centered, Lisa would then get three glasses of ice water, which she lined up across the top of her tray. If any liquid (water, juice) spilled onto the tray, she would begin again. Once the tray had been organized, Lisa sat with her friends and ate. Once she had consumed three of the five pieces of food and all of the water, she pushed her tray away and commented how full she was and that she couldn't believe she had eaten so much.

Mr. and Mrs. Baker recognized that Lisa had lost weight but stated, "She was always a little chunky and now she looks quite attractive." The Bakers reported that Lisa was the youngest of five girls and had always been their "angel." Lisa had always earned As in school, was a cheerleader in high school, was on the student council, and was elected homecoming queen her senior year. While her grades from college had not arrived, they were confident she had earned all As.

Once her parents had left, Lisa seemed willing to answer the therapist's questions. Lisa also recognized that she had lost a significant amount of weight and stated that she felt she still needed to lose 5 to 10 more pounds because her stomach was fat. When the therapist responded that Lisa did not look fat, Lisa reported that was why she wore sweats. The oversized sweats hid all her fat.

Lisa reported that if she could just lose the weight, her life would be much better. She was pledging a sorority in the spring and her future sorority sisters did not like fat girls. In addition, the guys at the university had begun asking her out as the weight dropped.

When questioned, Lisa reported that she was majoring in business because her parents felt that she would make more money with that major. She was sure all of her grades would be As, because ". . . college isn't that hard." While she was able to report that her eating habits were unusual, she stated that ". . . all diets are weird. It's the only way I can prevent myself from overeating. I think about food all the time."

Lisa also reported that she jogged 2 to 3 miles each day and rode an exercise bike in the dorm each evening for an hour. She reported that she had begun to ride around 2 A.M. to prevent the dorm counselor from catching her. Lisa reported that she had not had a period in three months although she knew she couldn't be pregnant because she was a virgin.

Possible Diagnosis and Treatment Options

CASE 20   *Patrick*

Patrick Callahan was first introduced to the therapist while guest lecturing for a colleague at a community college. Patrick was a tall, lanky, ten-year-old Caucasian with a baseball cap covering his straight black hair. His mother and father had brought him to the lecture because they were interested in the therapist answering questions about what they perceived as "odd" behavior on their son's part.

After the lecture, the Callahans cornered the therapist next to the refreshments and began asking questions about children who experienced problems sleeping. Mrs. Callahan was interested in whether it was unusual for children to walk in their sleep. The therapist reassured her that many individuals walk and talk in their sleep and, by itself, these behaviors did not suggest a serious psychological problem. Mr. Callahan then joined the conversation, asking what would constitute a serious problem. At this point, the therapist became concerned as to whether the Callahans were discussing problems that Patrick might be having, especially as Patrick was blushing furiously and trying to pull his parents away from the therapist. The therapist suggested that any time parents were concerned about a child's sleeping habits, a talk with their physician or with a psychologist would be the best way to resolve any doubts. As suspected, the Callahans reported that their physician had suggested that they discuss Patrick's sleeping problems with a psychologist. An appointment was made for the following week.

The Callahans arrived for the appointment on time. Patrick once again wore his baseball cap. Mr. and Mrs. Callahan were interviewed first while Patrick waited in the play room. Mr. Callahan was a sixth-grade teacher in the local elementary school and Mrs. Callahan worked as a secretary in the same school. Patrick was their only son. From the age of five, Patrick would awaken at night and wander the house. These sleepwalking incidents usually occurred once or twice a month and were of only minor concern, as Patrick did not attempt to leave the house and had never been injured. Over the past two years, the sleepwalking incidents had increased in frequency, and a new problem had emerged. Approximately two years before seeking help, Patrick had awakened his parents with bloodcurdling screams. Mr. and Mrs. Callahan had rushed to his room to find Patrick sitting up in bed and screaming. He appeared very frightened. Mr. Callahan had attempted to awaken his son by shaking him and calling his name. Eventually Patrick awoke, but seemed surprised to see his parents and could not remember having a bad dream or screaming. The following morning, Patrick had no memory of the incident. Mr. Callahan reported that he had attributed this incident to a bad nightmare. Unfortunately, Patrick continued to have such incidents two to three times a week for the next three months. Just when the Callahans had decided to seek help, the incidents decreased in frequency to once or twice a month. This continued for approximately nine months when the incidents once again increased in frequency to two to three times a week. Just as in the previous year, the incidents decreased to once or twice a month after about three months. For the past nine months, the incidents had been infrequent. However, the past week had seen Patrick once again experiencing the episodes two to three times a week. The previous weekend Patrick had refused to attend a sleepover at his best friend's house because he was scared that he might have one of his "fits." At this point, the Callahans had called their physician who had recommended a therapist.

The Callahans reported that in all other respects, Patrick was a happy and healthy child. He was a happy baby who slept through the night by the time he was two months old. Developmental milestones were achieved within a normal age range. Currently, Patrick was in the fourth grade at the local elementary school where his parents worked. He earned As and Bs and interacted well with his peers. He played soccer, basketball, and baseball, although baseball was his favorite. Patrick was the star hitter for his Little League team. Mr. Callahan reported that he had played baseball in high school also.

When asked what was occurring in Patrick's life when these incidents began, the Callahans seemed stumped. Mrs. Callahan reported that the incidents usually began in early March and lasted until school was out. She questioned whether the "fits" could be due to being tired of school. Mr. Callahan mentioned that the year Patrick had begun having his "fits" was the first year he played Little League. Mr. Callahan denied that this could be a problem though as he and Patrick had played baseball in the back yard since Patrick was two. In addition, Patrick had played t-ball for years prior to beginning Little League baseball.

The therapist then asked whether their physician had discussed any physical problems that Patrick might be experiencing that could lead to these types of incidents. Mr. Callahan reported that their physician had told them that nothing was physically wrong with Patrick. When questioned about possible medications Patrick might be taking at this time of the year, such as allergy medications, the Callahans reported that Patrick had no allergies and was only given acetaminophen on occasion.

Patrick came into the playroom slowly. He questioned the therapist about his parents not being in the room but seemed unconcerned about the therapist's response. Patrick sat against the couch, tossing a ball into the air and catching it as he responded to questions. Patrick reported that his parents were upset about his sleepwalking and his nightmares. When asked if these episodes upset him, Patrick grimaced and reported that the incidents did not upset him. However, he was embarrassed about them and did not want his friends to find out.

Patrick reported much of the same information that his parents had reported. He stated that his favorite subject at school was science and his least favorite was spelling. He enjoyed riding his bike, playing soccer, swimming, going to movies, and playing baseball. He reported that his best friends were Eric and Paul and that both of them were on his Little League baseball team.

When asked what he liked most about his parents, Patrick paused for close to five minutes. Finally, he reported that his Mom was a great cook and that all the other kids liked his Dad. When asked what things he did not like about his parents, Patrick's answer was instantaneous. Patrick reported that he hated his Dad always questioning him about baseball and telling him he wasn't trying hard enough. When the question was repeated in relation to his Mom, Patrick stated that he wished his Mom wouldn't act so disappointed in him when he messed up at the baseball games.

Patrick went on to report that his parents were great in that they were always willing to take him to games and let him try any sport he wanted. Neither of his parents knew much about swimming or soccer. However, since his Dad had played baseball, he was always telling him to do something different in order to improve his game. When asked why Patrick didn't tell his parents how he felt, Patrick rolled his eyes and replied that he didn't want his parents to take him out of baseball.

Possible Diagnosis and Treatment Options

CASE **21**   *Joe and Erin*

Joe and Erin Hunter were referred to the psychologist by the Department of Child Welfare in their state. The social worker who contacted the psychologist reported that the childrens' teachers had contacted the Department after Erin came to school with a black eye, which, according to Erin's report to her classmates, was given to her by her father. The social worker reported that she had gone to the school and interviewed the teachers and both Joe and Erin.

Erin, aged ten, was a fourth grader at a local elementary and her brother, aged twelve, was a sixth grader at the same school. Their teachers, Ms. Daniels and Ms. Baker, taught Joe and Erin respectively. They reported that the Hunter children were well-behaved and excellent students. Joe tended to be a class leader and was a gifted athlete. Erin was quieter than her brother, never volunteering to answer questions or join any activity. Both children received straight As and had never been in trouble at school. The teachers were surprised by Erin's claim that her father had hit her. Erin was not known as a liar, but both teachers had met Mr. and Mrs. Hunter and had found them to be polite, hardworking, and concerned parents. Both of the Hunters attended school events and parent-teacher conferences. The teachers reported that Erin and Joe frequently came to school with bruises or scratches but that wasn't unusual with children, especially with Joe, who was so active in sports.

Erin was interviewed first in the principal's office. Erin told the social worker that she had lied to her friends so that she would be more exciting. Erin reported that the black eye had occurred because her brother, Joe, had thrown a baseball that accidentally hit her in the eye. Erin reported no problems with her parents or with her brother. The social worker noted several burn marks on Erin's arm and neck that appeared to be from cigarettes. Erin reported that these marks were caused by mosquito bites. The social worker then photographed the visible burns and Erin's eye.

Next, the social worker met with Joe. According to Joe, Erin's black eye was due to her running into her bedroom door that morning. Joe reported that Erin was very clumsy. He also noted no problems with his mother, father, or sister.

After discussion with the supervisor, it was decided that the children would be removed from the home until an investigation was completed. The presence of the burns, the black eye, and the conflicting stories were suspicious enough for the social worker and the supervisor to be concerned about the safety of the children. Over the course of the following week, the court authorized a therapist to interview the children to help determine if the children had been abused and, if so, by whom.

Erin was seen by the therapist first, allowing Joe to remain in the waiting room with the social worker. Erin had long blond hair and green eyes. She was of average height for her age but weighed less than would have been expected. She was dressed in clean blue jeans, designer tennis shoes, and t-shirt. Her black eye and burns were still very evident.

The therapist took Erin into the playroom where all sessions were videotaped. Erin stayed by the door as the therapist entered the room and sat on the floor. Erin was encouraged to enter the room and play with whatever she wanted. Reluctantly, Erin entered the room and picked up a Barbie on the far side of the room. When asked why she thought she was there, Erin reported that she was in trouble. When asked why she might be in trouble, Erin refused to answer but began playing with the Barbie. Erin was willing to talk about her favorite toys (Barbies and rollerblades), her favorite show (anything on Nickelodeon), and her friends. As she talked, she brought her Barbie and sat across from the therapist on the floor. When asked about her mom, Erin hesitated, then said that she loved her mom very much, but that she had to work all the time. Erin reported that her mother worked at a local restaurant from 3 P.M. to midnight. Because of her schedule, Erin only got to see her mom on weekends and holidays. Erin went on to report that her brother watched her until their dad got home around 4:30 from his job. When asked about her dad, Erin started twisting her Barbie and refused to answer anymore questions.

Erin was taken back to the waiting room and Joe was brought back. Joe was tall and quite muscular for a twelve-year-old. He wore blue jeans, expensive tennis shoes, and a polo shirt. He glared angrily at the therapist from the doorway of the playroom. When encouraged to play with any toy, Joe stomped into the room and flung himself down into a chair. He immediately told the therapist that his sister Erin was clumsy and a liar. When asked why Erin would lie to her friends or the therapist, Joe scowled and stated that Erin enjoyed being the center of attention. The therapist switched the topic asking Joe what types of sports he enjoyed. Joe looked suspicious but reluctantly began talking about his love of soccer, basketball, and baseball. He was looking forward to seventh grade when he could begin playing football, too. When questioned about school, Joe reported that school was great. He said he enjoyed his classes, especially math and science, and said that he wanted to be a doctor when he grew up. When asked why he wanted to be a doctor, Joe responded that doctors were rich and refused to answer any other questions.

Given the responses of the children and the seriousness of the possible abuse, it was decided that Erin and Joe would meet with the therapist twice a week. In addition, with the permission of the court, the therapist would be allowed to interview the parents. Finally, upon the recommendation of the social worker and with the approval of the therapist, the court agreed to return the children to their home. This return was conditional on the father moving out of the home until the court decided whether charges of abuse were to be filed. The father agreed to these conditions and the children were returned to their mother.

Over the course of the next four months, the therapist met with Erin and Joe twice a week after school. It quickly became apparent that both children loved their parents tremendously and were happy to be back home with their mother. Both felt guilty about their father being out of the house and the fact that they could only see their father while the social worker was in the room.

Over the course of these sessions with the children, Erin developed a strong bond with the therapist, frequently hugging the therapist at the beginning and end of each session. Joe, too, became less hostile and more open with the therapist. Joe reported that his Dad had begun getting angry a few months before their Mom took the job at the restaurant. Joe had heard them arguing about money for months but was too little (age seven) to understand the problem, and besides, they were always bought nice clothes, toys, and went out to eat at least once a week at a nice restaurant. Once Mom went to work, Joe reported that his Dad became more and more angry. After work, he would become angry if Joe and Erin did not have dinner ready or if their homework wasn't done. At first, he would yell at them and spank them on the bottom. Within about six months, he had hit Joe in the face with his fist and thrown Erin against a wall when she dropped a glass of milk. Over the past year, Joe reported that his Dad became angry at the littlest things. The burns on Erin's arms occurred because she failed to complete all of her math homework before her Dad got home. Erin had received one burn for each math problem she hadn't completed. Joe had tried to explain that Erin had already finished her science assignment and learned all of her spelling words but his Dad had simply slapped him for interfering. Joe reported that his Dad wasn't "bad," but something was "hurting" him. When asked why Joe and Erin had not told their teachers before, Joe reported that he and Erin didn't want to get their Dad in trouble.

Erin confirmed her brother's reports with her own stories. After about eight weeks of meeting with the therapist, Erin was playing with a doll when tears began rolling down her face. She reported that she loved her Dad but that sometimes he became very angry when she and Joe misbehaved. She reported that the night before she had received the black eye she had dropped two plates full of food and that her father had hit her in the eye. Erin reported that her father immediately apologized and that he didn't mean to hurt her. When questioned about the burns, Erin shrugged, and said that she wasn't a "good girl." Erin reported that her Dad had always lost his temper when she or Joe misbehaved.

The therapist met with the Hunters approximately ten weeks after the initial meeting with Joe and Erin. Mr. Hunter was about thirty-five years of age, dressed in a navy pinstripe suit. Mrs. Hunter, also about thirty-five, was dressed in a casual skirt and sweater. The Hunters entered the room tentatively. The therapist began the session by thanking Mr. Hunter for moving out of his home. Both of the Hunters seemed astonished by this statement. Mr. Hunter, recovering first, commented that he was relieved that the therapist wasn't going to accuse him of abusing his children. The therapist went on to explain that her job was to determine why the problems had occurred and to get Mr. Hunter back into the home.

The Hunters reported that they had been married for fourteen years. Mr. Hunter worked in a local bank and Mrs. Hunter was a manager of a local restaurant. Mrs. Hunter reported that she began working two years ago when her husband had lost his job as a result of downsizing. Although he had found another job at a bank, money had been very tight for a while and they were still trying to pay off some of their debts. Mrs. Hunter reported that she didn't mind working but that she'd like to return to college so she would be able to have a job in her area of interest, teaching.

The Hunters both described their children in positive terms. Both of them attended parent-teacher conferences and went to all of Joe's games they could. Mrs. Hunter expressed concern about how quiet Erin was but noted that she seemed to be opening up more since she had been coming to see the therapist.

Mrs. Hunter stopped talking in mid-sentence and stared directly at the therapist. She asked in a very firm tone if the therapist believed her husband had abused Joe and Erin. Before the therapist could answer, Mr. Hunter responded to his wife's question. Mr. Hunter turned to his wife and gently moved her chin so that she faced him. He quietly told her that he had hit the children and that he had even burned Erin with a cigarette.

Mrs. Hunter turned white and began crying. Mr. Hunter told the therapist that he needed help as he didn't want to lose his wife and children. He admitted that he had always believed that spanking was okay but that lately it seemed to be getting out of hand. He reported that he was embarrassed when the social worker had removed Erin and Joe and had tried to blame everyone else. Over the past weeks, he had become more and more upset as he saw his children and wife living without him.

Possible Diagnosis and Treatment Options

Section 2
DIAGNOSIS AND CONCEPTUALIZATION

CASE 1   *Natasha*

Diagnosis: Mental Retardation, Mild

In cases of suspected mental retardation, three criteria must be met to arrive at a diagnosis. Criterion B is especially important given the history of the misuse of intelligence testing in this country (see Gould, 1981, for a discussion of this issue).

A. Onset must be before the age of 18
B. Age-appropriate adaptive functioning must be impaired in at least two of the following areas: communication, self-care, home living, social/interpersonal skills, use of community resources, self-direction, functional academic skills, work, leisure, health, and safety
C. Intellectual functioning must be significantly subaverage, which is defined as an IQ of below 70 on a standard, individually administered IQ test

Various degrees of mental retardation should also be assessed. Severity is typically defined by IQ level but corresponds to behavioral impairments:

Mild—approximately 50–55 up to 69
Moderate—approximately 35–40 up to 50–55
Severe—approximately 20–25 up to 35–40
Profound—below 20–25

Discussion

There is no treatment for Natasha's mental retardation. While some types of retardation can be treated or prevented (PKU, for example), this is not true for the majority of individuals who are mentally retarded. In addition, there is no clear reason for Natasha's mental retardation. In many cases, some etiological factor can be identified; however, in approximately 35 percent of cases, no clear etiology can be determined. Given the lack of treatment to correct or "cure" Natasha's mental retardation, the therapist's goal is to help Natasha, her parents, and her school create the best long-term circumstances for Natasha.

In a case such as Natasha's, the primary goals of treatment are twofold. First, Natasha needs education appropriate for her speed of learning to improve her skills to the maximum level possible. Natasha will be continued in school even though she will never achieve at the same level as the other children. For Natasha, social development is as important as the academic skills she is gaining. Second, care should be taken not to allow the name calling engaged in by the other children to progress to the point where Natasha's self-esteem will suffer. While medication has been used with some cases of mental retardation, the decision was made not to use medication in Natasha's case. Haloperidol (Haldol) is useful in reducing aggression but Natasha did not exhibit aggressive tendencies. Although stimulant medication has been found effective in some cases of mental retardation, the potential side effects and questionable efficacy were of concern to Natasha's parents. Instead, Natasha's case was handled by using behavioral skills training aimed at independent living and a tailored approach to supplemental education.

Working with Natasha's principal, teacher, and special education teacher was seen as critical for successfully achieving Natasha's maximum performance. After much discussion, Natasha remained in her regular classroom for most of the day. She left the classroom for special education in reading and math. In addition, the special education teacher worked with Natasha's classroom teacher to design appropriate assignments for Natasha. The special education teacher also supplied a trained aide to the classroom teacher who would help supervise Natasha and other learning disabled children in the classroom.

Natasha's parents enrolled Natasha in a specialized enrichment class for mildly mentally retarded students offered by the school on Saturday mornings. This course was designed by the school psychologist to teach practical skills to these children. Children learned to cook simple meals (e.g., macaroni and cheese), buy simple items with cash (e.g., Christmas presents), read a bus schedule, vote, and other life skills. Natasha thrived in this environment and was able to tie her own shoes within a month.

By the time Natasha entered sixth grade, her adaptive skills had improved so that she was able to blend within the range of the other children. Her reading and math skills were still significantly behind the majority of her peers and were tested at the third to fourth grade level. She was allowed to enter sixth grade despite her failure to achieve to grade level and adjusted well to the middle school. Natasha continued to receive assistance from the special education teachers until she graduated from high school. In Natasha's school, a special diploma was issued for those children in special education that acknowledged their accomplishments while also noting that they had not completed all of the requirements for regular high school graduation. Upon graduation, Natasha worked in a local factory for two years prior to marrying and having children.

CASE 2   *Joey*

Diagnosis: Autistic Disorder

In order to diagnose Autistic Disorder, the therapist must differentiate between other Pervasive Developmental Disorders, including Rett's Disorder, Asperger's Disorder, and Childhood Disintegrative Disorder. Rett's Disorder has presently been diagnosed only in females. Since Joey is male, this would make a diagnosis of Rett's highly unlikely. In addition, in Rett's Disorder, there is a pattern of head growth deceleration, loss of previously acquired hand skills, and the appearance of poorly coordinated gait or trunk movements. Joey does not demonstrate these characteristics, effectively eliminating Rett's Disorder from consideration.

In Asperger's Disorder, there is no delay in language development. Given Joey's language difficulties, Asperger's does not fit and must be eliminated. Finally, in Childhood Disintegrative Disorder, there must be at least two (2) years of normal development prior to a regression. In Joey's case, it is not possible to document two years of normal development.

Therefore, the best diagnosis for Joey would be Autistic Disorder. According to the DSM-IV, three criteria must be met:

A. Six or more items from 1, 2, and 3 with at least two items from 1, and one item each from 2 and 3
   1. Social Interaction impairments:
      a. Nonverbal behaviors markedly impaired (e.g., eye-to-eye gaze, facial expression, body postures, gestures)
      b. No age-appropriate peer relationships
      c. Lack of spontaneous seeking to share enjoyment, interests, or achievements with others
      d. Fails to respond socially or emotionally
   2. Communication impairments:
      a. Delay in, or total lack, of spoken language (child must not be attempting to communicate through gestures)
      b. Impairments in initiating or sustaining a conversation

      c. Language that is stereotyped, repetitive, or idiosyncratic

      d. Lack of vivid, spontaneous make-believe play or age-appropriate social imitative play

   3. Restricted repetitive and stereotyped patterns of behavior, interests, or activities:

      a. Preoccupation with one or more stereotyped and restricted patterns of interest that is abnormal in intensity or focus

      b. Inflexible adherence to specific, nonfunctional routines or rituals

      c. Stereotyped and repetitive motor mannerisms

      d. May be preoccupied with parts of objects

B. Delays or abnormal functioning in at least one of the following with onset prior to age three:

   1. Social interaction

   2. Social communication

   3. Play involving imagination or symbols

C. Must not be due to Rett's Disorder or Childhood Disintegrative Disorder

Discussion

Following the initial session with Joey and his parents, the parents took Joey to a physician who agreed with the diagnosis of autism. Joey was found to have bruising about his head from his episodes of head banging. No other medical problems were found.

A meeting with Ms. Small, Joey's preschool teacher, was quite productive. Ms. Small confirmed the statements by the Bowens and expressed considerable concern that Joey had not been under the care of professionals before. She was hesitant to allow Joey to return to preschool as she believed it was not productive for Joey or the other children. It was agreed that Joey would be removed from preschool for the remainder of the year. Ms. Small also agreed to consider having Joey in preschool the following year based on his success in treatment.

Joey was brought to the therapist the following week when he was videotaped while in a playroom. This observation along with the interview data allowed a more complete assessment of the particular areas in which Joey demonstrated deficits. As noted above, Joey's communication problems were of primary concern. His head banging, temper tantrums, and refusal to be touched were also seen as prime obstacles to successful treatment.

At this point, the therapist believed sufficient assessment of Joey and his family had been done to initiate treatment. Although many cases of autism do not improve, Joey's case seemed hopeful to the therapist because of his response to the book. Treatment would necessitate an enormous commitment of time and energy from the Bowens. Even if this time and energy were given, no guarantee could be made about the long-term prognosis of Joey's case. After explaining these issues to the Bowens, they decided they would like Joey treated and that Mrs. Bowen would be the primary contact with the treatment team. In addition to the treatment for Joey, the Bowens were offered supportive marital counseling. The stress of Joey's disorder appeared to be negatively affecting the Bowens's relationship. The Bowens eagerly accepted the offer of marital counseling and appeared to thrive as a result of this aid.

The therapist began Joey in a structured therapy program modeled after Lovaas's (Lovaas & Smith, 1989) program. This program involves a daily treatment schedule aimed at shaping and reinforcing desired behaviors while punishing undesired behavior. Although other treatments have been tried (see, for example, Yarbrough, Santat, Perel, & Webster, et. al., 1987), none have been demonstrated to be as effective as the behavior modification procedures outlined by Lovaas. Mrs. Bowen agreed to be trained in the program as well in order to be able to maintain the program at home and to ensure generalization of treatment gains away from the clinic setting. For the first six months, Joey came to the clinic each day from 9 A.M. to 5 P.M. Volunteers trained in the treatment method served as Joey's therapists. It was quickly discovered that Joey loved books and food and would work to earn these privileges. His noises were discovered to be attempts to make contact with others and were reinforced and then shaped until he began using words. Negative behaviors were also addressed. Although some studies have found certain medications such as antipsychotics effective in reducing or eliminating self-mutilating behavior and stereotypies, behavioral techniques were utilized with Joey first because of the high probability of negative side effects with such medications. Head banging was found to occur only during the night. During the first six months of the program, Joey wore a protective helmet to bed each night. Joey did not like the helmet and would frequently throw temper tantrums and try to get the helmet off. Once Joey had developed some language capacity, his parents and his therapist explained to him that if he banged his head, he would wear the helmet. After six months, Joey was allowed to sleep without the helmet. The first night, he banged his head, which led to his parents immediately replacing the helmet. The next night Joey did not bang his head. Over the course of the following six months, Joey's head banging stopped completely.

As Joey's language skills improved and his negative behaviors decreased, Mrs. Bowen became more active as a therapist for her son. Over the second six months, Joey continued to come to the clinic on the same daily schedule but now his mother served as his therapist, with supervision, in the afternoons. In addition, Joey was enrolled in a Mother's Day Out program one morning a week. This was done to allow Joey exposure to other children and to increase generalization of treatment effects. Prior to enrolling Joey, the therapist worked with the director and the teachers of this program to prepare them for Joey. Joey attended for two hours each week. The first week Joey attended the teachers arranged for reading to occur while Joey was there increasing the odds that Joey would have a positive experience. Over the course of this second six months, Joey had one temper tantrum at the Mother's Day Out. Rocking also occurred on two occasions. Although Joey did not talk very much during these play times, he did tell two other boys his name and told them his favorite show was *Power Rangers*.

After the first year, Ms. Small agreed to take Joey back into preschool as long as he continued treatment. During this second year of treatment, Joey came to the clinic only in the afternoons. Most of the focus of treatment during this second year was on social interaction and language. During the third year, Joey discontinued treatment at the clinic and continued home treatment with his mother as his therapist. In addition, Joey was placed into a regular kindergarten class at his local public elementary school.

The therapist recontacted the Bowens when Joey was in the fourth grade. The parents reported that Joey was still in a regular classroom (earning mainly Bs with an occasional A) and the teachers were unaware that Joey had been diagnosed with autism. While Joey continued to be quieter than his peers, he had recently received a B in conduct for talking too much in class. The Bowens reported that Joey still preferred to spend most of his time alone but had two good friends. In addition, Joey now had twin sisters who were four. The girls had been seen by their family physician regularly and showed no signs of any psychological problems.

CASE 3   *Jimmy*

Diagnosis: Attention Deficit Hyperactivity Disorder

Diagnosing a child with Attention Deficit Hyperactivity Disorder (ADHD) is a task that requires careful consideration. Over the past ten to fifteen years, this disorder has become the common cold of childhood psychopathology. Therapists and parents need to be careful not to assume a child is truly suffering from ADHD on the basis of a teacher's or a parent's report. It is critical to remember that the DSM-IV requires documentation of symptoms in at least two separate settings. Physicians also need to be very careful not to diagnose a child as suffering from ADHD based solely on a parent's subjective reports of their child's behavior. A careful assessment of the child by a qualified psychologist is the first step to successfully ameliorating the problems associated with this condition. In the present case, there was clear documentation of Jimmy's problems in the home, in the therapist's office, and in the school. Frequently, however, cases are not as clear as the case of Jimmy. Many children with ADHD can perform extremely well in the therapist's office, as this type of one-on-one contact enables them to focus their activity in a more acceptable manner. Because of this, a school or home visit may be critical to accurately diagnosing a child with ADHD.

According to the DSM-IV, ADHD is only diagnosed when the following conditions and / or symptoms are present:

A. Symptoms leading to impairment present before the age of seven
B. Documented impairment in two or more settings
C. Clear evidence of clinically significant impairment in social, academic, or occupational functioning
D. Symptoms do not occur exclusively during the course of another mental disorder
E. Either 1. or 2. below:
    1. Child must exhibit six or more of the following symptoms of inattention that have persisted for at least six months and are maladaptive and are not developmentally appropriate

    a. Poor attention to detail; makes careless mistakes in schoolwork, work, or other activities

    b. Difficulty sustaining attention

    c. Fails to listen even when spoken to directly

    d. Fails to complete work or instructions, but not as a result of a lack of understanding or oppositional behavior

    e. Organizational difficulties

    f. Often avoids, dislikes, or is reluctant to engage in tasks requiring sustained mental activity

    g. Often loses things

    h. Easily distracted

    i. Forgetful

2. Child must exhibit six or more of the following symptoms of hyperactivity or impulsivity that have persisted for at least six months and are maladaptive and are not developmentally appropriate

Hyperactivity

    a. Often fidgets or squirms in seat

    b. Can't sit for long periods of time; gets out of seat

    c. Often runs about or climbs excessively in inappropriate situations

    d. Difficulty playing or engaging in leisure activities quietly

    e. Often "on the go" or described as "driven by a motor"

    f. Often talks excessively

Impulsivity

    g. Blurts out answers before the question has been completed

    h. Difficulty awaiting turns

    i. Often interrupts or intrudes on others

Discussion

Given the extensive literature on the treatment of this disorder (see for example, Engeland, 1993), the therapist decided that a combination pharmacological and behavioral treatment approach would be most effective in this case. These treatments appear to work well in combination and provide both immediate relief of the symptoms and long-term reinforcement of positive behavior. This approach was also viewed as one that would be most acceptable to Jimmy, his parents, and his teacher. While this should never be a prime consideration in treatment selection, it is fortunate when the most effective approach also happens to be one which would have high acceptance for the participants in the program.

    With the parents' approval, Jimmy's physician was contacted and appraised of Jimmy's diagnosis of ADHD. After discussion of Jimmy's symptoms, the physician made the decision to place Jimmy on Ritalin (methyl-phenidate). Jimmy would receive one dose prior to going to school and one dose at lunchtime that would be given by school authorities.

Ms. Hall was pleased that Jimmy would be calmer in the classroom and agreed to work with the therapist in helping to manage Jimmy's problematic behaviors. A classroom management procedure was developed, using behavioral principles, tailored to the types of problems Jimmy was experiencing (e.g., getting out of his seat) and what Ms. Hall saw as reasonable methods of addressing the situation. Given that Jimmy and his sisters would be attending the same school for the next six years, it was considered critical to accommodate the school as much as possible.

Finally, the parents were educated about ADHD and the role of Ritalin in the treatment of the disorder. After the Conners understood the nature of the disorder, their behavioral checklists were used to design behavioral procedures to address problem areas in the home. The Conners were pleased with Jimmy's improvement on the Ritalin and with the simple procedures they learned to use with Jimmy. Mr. Conner suggested, and implemented, a "boy's night out" once a week to reward Jimmy for his improved behavior.

The therapist continued to work with the parents on a weekly basis and the teacher on a monthly basis until the winter break. In January, the parents and therapist decided weekly meetings were no longer needed and reduced meetings to once a month. By the end of the school year, the Conners felt comfortable having no further sessions. The teacher continued to call the therapist throughout the second half of the school year but believed Jimmy's behavior was now "just that of a rambunctious child." However, Ms. Hall asked for, and received, permission to forward the therapist's name to Jimmy's second-grade teacher. The therapist did not receive calls from Jimmy's second-grade teacher.

The physician reported that Jimmy was maintained on Ritalin throughout the school year and was given a medication break during the summer. This pattern was continued throughout Jimmy's elementary years. Jimmy's medication was discontinued when he entered eighth grade. No negative effects were reported by Jimmy, his parents, or his teachers when the medication was discontinued.

CASE 4   *Randall*

Diagnosis: Oppositional Defiant Disorder
               Attention Deficit Hyperactivity Disorder

    Rule Out: Conduct Disorder

In Randall's case, the biggest considerations in terms of diagnosing involve his previous diagnosis of ADHD and the possibility of Conduct Disorder. Randall was taking his Ritalin throughout the assessment process. It is the belief of Randall, his teachers, and his parents that his behavior was worse when he did not take his medication. Taking Randall off the medication at this time does not seem warranted. However, Randall's present behavior does not confirm ADHD. In looking at the criteria for a diagnosis of ADHD (see Case 3, Jimmy), Randall fails to meet these criteria. It is not unusual for children to exhibit both ADHD and Oppositional Defiant Disorder, however, and, in the absence of being able to assess Randall without the presence of Ritalin, this diagnosis appears to make the most sense. Likewise, Randall shows similar behavior to that needed for a diagnosis of Conduct Disorder (see Case 5, Scott). However, the level of Randall's behavior is not as aggressive nor as confrontational as seen in Conduct Disorder. Many psychologists believe that Oppositional Defiant Disorder is simply a less severe form of Conduct Disorder.

It might seem odd that Randall was essentially compliant with the requests of the examiner in light of his behavior at school and in the home. However, clinicians frequently note that children exhibiting these symptoms are more likely to experience problems with adults and children they know well.

Randall's behavioral problems most closely follow the criteria of Oppositional Defiant Disorder, which are outlined as follows:

A. Characterized by a pattern of behavior, of at least six months' duration, including negativistic, hostile, and defiant behavior in which four (4) or more of the following are included:

1. Frequently loses temper
2. Frequently argues with adults
3. Actively defies or refuses to comply with the demands of adults
4. Frequently annoys people on purpose
5. Frequently blames others for his or her own mistakes
6. Frequently annoyed by others
7. Frequently angry or resentful
8. Frequently spiteful or resentful

B. These behavioral problems lead to clinically significant disruptions in daily functioning

Discussion

The use of a parent-training approach was determined to be the best choice for Randall and his parents. Parent training has been found effective in cases of Oppositional Defiant Disorder and was acceptable to Randall's parents. Individual psychotherapy was considered but rejected because of the high relapse rate associated with this approach.

The Ellises joined a parent-training group, led by the psychologist, that focused on the use of behavioral strategies and psychoeducational in nature. Parents in the group are taught specific behavioral techniques that increase the likelihood of maintaining control of the child. Gradual shaping of the child's behavior to be more age-appropriate is accomplished through the use of a behavioral monitoring and reward program.

The Ellises selected Randall's hitting as one of the first behaviors they wished to address. Rather than spanking Randall each time he hit one of his siblings, a plan was developed involving loss of privileges. The most important activities and personal items of Randall were identified. Each time Randall hit one of his siblings, one of these activities or items were lost for one day. The Ellises were enthusiastic during the development of the plan but, after the first week, reported that the implementation of the plan was more work than they had expected. Other group members were able to share with the Ellises the eventual positive outcomes they had experienced by adhering to the plan despite the increased effort. Over the course of the next seven weeks, Randall decreased his hitting in the home significantly. Additional problematic behaviors were addressed one at a time. The therapist discovered that the Ellises tended to be quite strict with their children. At some points, the Ellises were encouraged to reevaluate their rules and to allow Randall more autonomy. During this time, increased chances for positive interactions between Randall and his parents, individually and together, were also planned.

The problems Randall was having at school also needed to be addressed. The therapist, along with the school psychologist and Randall's teacher, developed a behavioral plan for use during the school day. The most disturbing behaviors to the teacher were the class disruptions (including passing gas and head banging), rude comments, and Randall's loud tone of voice. Both the school psychologist and the teacher acknowledged that they would threaten Randall with expulsion but did not actually expel him. It was decided that in-school suspension would be used instead of the threat of expulsion. A plan was developed allowing the teacher to give Randall three blue cards each day. If Randall received three blue cards, he would immediately be sent to the principal's office where he would complete the remainder of his school work in an isolated room. If the third blue card was given after 2 P.M., Randall would spend the entire next school day in the isolated room. On days when Randall received fewer than three blue cards, Randall would be allowed to choose a book from the teacher's collection of books that were given to children for positive behavior.

Randall was skeptical of the program when it was explained to him. On the first day, he earned all three blue cards within twenty minutes. When asked to go to the principal's office, Randall knocked his desk over and stomped out of the room. On the next day, Randall again earned all three blue cards within thirty minutes. This time he quietly left the room when requested. On the third day of the program, Randall did not earn his third blue card until after lunch. He became visibly upset when the teacher gave him the third card and left the room before the teacher could ask him to do so. On the fourth day, Randall earned only two blue cards. Once school was over, the teacher allowed Randall to select a book. Randall spent close to fifteen minutes shifting through the stack of books until he finally made his decision. When he came to school on the fifth day of the program, Randall told his teacher that he had already read the book and asked if there was a sequel. Over the course of the next four months, Randall was able to earn a book approximately two times a week for the first nine weeks and then about three times a week for the remainder of the year. One unanticipated side effect of the program was that other children began to ask Randall which books they should choose to check out in the library. At the end of the school year, Randall continued to antagonize many of the girls in his class by making rude noises and poking them in the back or arm. His rudeness toward the teacher and the number of class disruptions decreased drastically. In addition, Randall's grades improved to all Bs and Cs.

At the end of the sixth grade, Randall was demonstrating more appropriate behavior both at home and at school. During the summer, Randall's Ritalin was discontinued. Randall and his parents reported no increase in problems as a result of the discontinuation of the medication over the summer. A meeting was held with Randall, his parents, the therapist, and the physician to discuss whether Randall should be placed back on Ritalin at the start of seventh grade. Randall would be changing schools for seventh grade, entering the local junior high. Although Randall was somewhat apprehensive about his ability to perform well at school, he agreed to a four-week trial of no medication. During these first four weeks, the Ellises reported to the therapist their observations of Randall, brought in Randall's school work, and reported on their first parent-teacher conference. The Ellises reported that Randall continued to bump girls in the hallway but had made several new friends on the school newspaper. His teachers reported that Randall exhibited no unusual behavior and one teacher could not remember which child Randall was. Randall's school work showed a consistent pattern of Bs. At the end of the four-week period, it was decided, with Randall's agreement, that medication would be discontinued until further notice. Over the course of the year, the Ellises continued to attend parent-training group sessions aimed at improving their skills at addressing individual behaviors. Randall achieved Bs in the seventh grade and was not sent to the principal's office even once during the year. The Ellises discontinued attending the parent-training group sessions during the summer after Randall completed the seventh grade. The therapist did not receive any further information about Randall.

Scott

Diagnosis: Conduct Disorder, Childhood-Onset Type, Mild

Scott's current diagnosis must be Conduct Disorder because of his symptoms, which included intimidating the other children and stealing their money, repeated lies to avoid obligations, and running away from home. Given that Scott demonstrated at least one of these criteria before the age of ten, childhood-onset type was specified. At this point, Scott's conduct disorder can be said to be mild because his behavior has caused only minor harm to others. His fire setting, if allowed to continue, may eventually lead to a change from mild to moderate.

According to the DSM-IV, conduct disorder is diagnosed when:

A. The behavior leads to clinically significant impairments in social, academic, or occupational functioning, and

B. A pattern of behavior is seen in which the basic rights of others are violated or major age-appropriate social norms or rules are violated. This must be objectively demonstrated by the presence of three or more of the criteria listed below within the past twelve months. In addition, at least one of the criteria listed below must have been present within the past six months:

  1. Aggression to people or animals
     This may include:
     a. Bullying or threatening others
     b. Initiating physical fights
     c. The use of a weapon that might cause serious harm to another (e.g., a knife)
     d. and e. Physical cruelty to people or animals
     f. Forcing sexual activity on another
     g. Stealing while confronting the victim
  2. Destruction of property
     This may include:
     a. Deliberately setting fires with the intention of causing serious damage

    b. Deliberately destroying others' property (other than fire setting)
3. Deceitfulness or theft
    This may include:
    a. Breaking into someone's house, building, or car
    b. Frequent lies to obtain privileges or goods, or to avoid responsibilities
    c. Stealing items of little to no value without confronting the victim
4. Serious violations of rules
    This may include:
    a. Staying out at night despite parental warnings, beginning before adolescence
    b. Running away from home overnight at least twice or once if for a lengthy period of time

Discussion

While the therapist saw Scott's case as potentially salvageable, Scott's parents were not willing to pursue therapy past the initial evaluation. Scott was placed in a boarding school for "troubled boys" in another state. After three weeks at this school, Scott was expelled for burning down the dorm. Fortunately, none of the students were injured. Charges were pressed against Scott and he was sent to a group home for delinquent boys. He remained at this home for three months before he and two older boys ran away. The three were caught a few days after leaving the home when they attacked a homeless man, stealing his money ($4.85) and beating him. As a result of this crime, Scott was sent to a detention facility until his eighteenth birthday. The therapist heard no further information about Scott.

    In recent studies, several effective methods of treating children with problems such as Scott's have been identified. If a child is identified with Oppositional Defiant Disorder (a milder form of Conduct Disorder that typically precedes the development of Conduct Disorder), parent-training programs and cognitive-skills training programs used in combination have been found to effectively reduce problematic behavior (see, for example, Kazdin, 1995).

    Once these children reach adolescence or become chronic juvenile offenders, the parent-training approaches do not appear to be as successful. One exception to this might be the functional family therapy developed by Alexander and his colleagues (e.g., Morris, Alexander, and Waldron, 1988). In this approach, behavioral-social learning and cognitive-behavioral and family-systems perspectives are combined in a focus on the interpersonal processes of the family.

    Once the child has entered the juvenile system, most experts consider incarceration to be the least favorable approach because it seems to lead to higher recidivism rates. Alternatives might include restitution, intensive probation supervision, and wilderness programs. Restitution involves the youth being required to pay money or perform community service for the victim or the community. Intensive probation supervision includes more frequent supervision by a probation officer, the involvement of the family, and involvement of other social services such as job training. Wilderness programs have become quite popular as a result of their focus on individual development and group cooperation. Unfortunately, these alternatives to institutionalization have not been adequately evaluated.

The Teaching Family Model (Fixsen, Wolf, & Phillips, 1973) is one community-based program that has led to considerable research. In this behaviorally oriented program, youths live in a house with two trained teaching parents. While in the program, the adolescents show marked improvement. Unfortunately, once they leave this structured environment, the gains they have made are frequently lost.

CASE 6   *Eric*

Diagnosis: Encopresis, Secondary Type

Encopresis is diagnosed when it meets the following four criteria listed in the DSM-IV:

    A. Involuntary or voluntary repeated passage of feces in inappropriate places (e.g., soiling clothes or floor)

    B. Must occur at least one time per month for the past three months

    C. Child must be at least four years of age

    D. This behavior must not be caused solely by the physiological effects of a substance (e.g., laxatives) or a general medical condition. Constipation is excluded from this condition.

Secondary Type is diagnosed in Eric's case because his encopresis developed after a period of fecal continence.

Discussion

In this case, the child appeared to have no substantive problems other than the encopresis. While it would certainly have been possible to see Eric in therapy, the potential for Eric's viewing himself as psychologically disturbed had to be considered. In addition, while no constipation was reported, it was felt that a medical exam to rule out colon problems was warranted. Following a physician's report that no colon problems were present in this case, therapy was initiated with Eric's parents. The issue of constipation and colon problems is an important one with encopresis. Approximately 80 percent of children with this disorder will develop these problems. Therapists need to continuously evaluate these conditions throughout therapy and work with physicians to assure proper treatment.

    With both parents attending, a behavior-modification program was outlined in the first therapy session. The parents then returned home, explained the procedure to Eric and elicited his help in selecting reinforcers for the absence of "accidents." During the second therapy session, the completed behavior-modification program was reviewed by the clinician. Not surprisingly, Eric had chosen reading time as one of his top reinforcers. Once the program was acceptable, procedures were discussed for implementing the program in the home. At the third therapy session, Eric's parents reported that he had experienced no "accidents" in the past week. Procedures were discussed for dealing with probable future "accidents" and the next therapy session was scheduled for two weeks. At the fourth therapy session, Eric had experienced one "accident," but, because the parents were prepared, they were able to get right back on the program. A fifth therapy session was scheduled for three weeks. At the fifth therapy session, Eric had experienced no "accidents." A final call-in was scheduled for one month. At the one month call-in, Eric's mother reported no new "accidents" and that Eric had made a new friend at school.

CASE 7   *Sam*

Diagnosis: Obsessive-Compulsive Disorder
               Transient Tic Disorder

Diagnosing Sam with both Obsessive-Compulsive Disorder and Tic Disorder is necessary in this case, as he meets the criteria for both conditions. This decision must be based on the differences between tics seen in Tic Disorder and the type of tics that are compulsions. In Tic Disorder, tics are usually simplistic in nature and do not serve to reduce anxiety surrounding the object of the individual's obsession. In Sam's case, the therapist noted the facial tics from the time Sam entered the therapy room, leading to a hypothesis that they were unassociated with the obsession. This hypothesis seemed to be confirmed during discussions with Sam. The increase in facial tics when questioned about his school work does not suggest that the tics are part of this disorder as it is well documented that tics are exacerbated by stress.

According to the DSM-IV, Obsessive-Compulsive Disorder is diagnosed when five criteria are met:

A. Either obsessions or compulsions:
    Obsessions are defined as:
    1. Recurrent thoughts, impulses, or images that are ego-dystonic and intrusive
    2. Cannot be excessive worries about real-life events
    3. Individual attempts to suppress these obsessions with some other thought or action
    4. Individual recognizes that the obsessions are a product of their own mind (not implanted from an external source)
    Compulsions are defined as:
    1. Repetitive behaviors or mental actions that the individual feels driven to perform in response to an obsession or according to a rigid set of rules
    2. Must be aimed at preventing or reducing anxiety or some dreaded

consequence; however, these acts are not logically connected or are clearly excessive

B. Individual must recognize at some point during the disorder that these obsessions or compulsions are excessive or unreasonable; this criterion is not required in children

C. Obsessions must cause significant distress, take more than one hour each day, or significantly interfere with the individual's normal routine, occupational or academic functioning, or usual social activities or relationships

D. Must not be caused by another mental disorder

E. Must not be caused by the direct physiological effects of a substance or a general medical condition

For Transient Tic Disorder, the DSM-IV requires six criteria to be met:

A. Single or multiple motor or vocal tics have been observed

B. Tics must occur several times each day, nearly every day for at least four weeks but no longer than twelve consecutive months

C. Disturbance must cause marked distress or significant impairment in social, occupational, or other important areas of functioning

D. Must not be due to the direct physiological effects of a substance or a general medical condition

E. Criteria have never been met for Tourette's Disorder or Chronic Motor or Vocal Tic Disorder

Discussion

In Sam's case, his obsessive-compulsive disorder was clearly interfering with his academic success as well as impeding the formation of new friendships. While the disorder seemed to have become full-blown only since the beginning of ninth grade, it was clear that the disorder was an outgrowth of Sam's personality style. Therefore, it was considered important to combine pharmacological and cognitive-behavioral treatment. Pharmacological treatment has been demonstrated to lead to quick improvements in obsessive-compulsive symptoms (see, for example, Allen, Leonard, & Swedo, 1995). Unfortunately, relapse is high following cessation of the medication. Given Sam's natural style of "perfectionism," relapse was viewed as a high probability in this case. Cognitive-behavioral treatment, therefore, was instituted along with medication.

With the aid of a colleague in psychiatry, Sam was placed on clomipramine. This tricyclic antidepressant was chosen because of its demonstrated effectiveness and the low number of serious problems seen with children and adolescents. Following two weeks of medication, Sam was scheduled for weekly sessions with the therapist. At this point a drastic reduction was noted in the intensity of Sam's obsessive-compulsive symptoms. No change was noted in Sam's facial tics. Cognitive-behavioral treatment was instituted focusing on Sam's work habits. Specifically, over the course of eight weeks, Sam and the therapist developed and implemented an exposure and response prevention procedure. First, with Sam's help, those situations that led to the most anxiety were identified and described. This anxiety hierarchy was organized from those situations that were least anxiety-provoking to those that were most anxiety-provoking. Then Sam was taught various relaxation techniques including distraction techniques, meditation, and muscle relaxation. In Sam's case, he found a mixture of these techniques was most helpful in relaxing. Hypnotic techniques were attempted but led to increased anxiety for Sam. At this point the parents were recruited into therapy. The parents were taught how to intervene in Sam's rituals in the home. Starting with the least anxiety-provoking situation, Sam was prevented from engaging in his rituals in the therapist's office and then in the home. Once Sam was able to complete the task in a reasonable time without his rituals, he was able to move up to the next anxiety-provoking situation. Over the course of eight weeks, Sam was able to relax and give up the majority of his rituals.

At the end of eight weeks in cognitive-behavioral therapy, Sam's medication was tapered and discontinued. Sam's anxiety increased for two weeks but with continued cognitive-behavioral therapy, the anxiety was decreased. At the end of fourteen weeks of therapy, Sam's obsessive-compulsive symptoms were decreased significantly and were no longer of concern. Sam was completing his homework in a reasonable amount of time (varied from one to four hours per night depending upon the number of assignments) and had developed two new friendships. However, Sam's facial tics had not changed in frequency or intensity. At this point, Sam's family physician, the psychiatrist, and the therapist agreed that the facial tics should be treated separately with medication. Risperidone, a drug used in the treatment of motor tics, was administered. Before initiating the use of this drug, it was agreed that a trial of four weeks would be acceptable and that the drug would be discontinued if Sam experienced any side effects or if significant improvement was not noted. This extra caution was deemed important as Risperidone was a relatively new drug at the time but with some demonstrated success with motor tics. Within two weeks, facial tics had diminished to the point where they were no longer problematic. Monitoring of this medication was continued by the family physician. After four weeks of treatment, medication was discontinued with no significant increase in facial tics.

CASE 8   *Amanda*

Diagnosis: Social Phobia

Amanda's case is difficult to diagnose because she shows symptoms of both Social Phobia and Separation Anxiety Disorder. First, Amanda demonstrates a disruption in her everyday functioning. The formation of peer relationships in her neighborhood and her school is essentially nonexistent. When confronted with feared situations, Amanda responds with tears, avoidance, and somatic symptoms, such as her vomiting on the school bus. The interaction, and seeming dependence, of Amanda and her mother calls into question the diagnosis of Separation Anxiety Disorder. However, no indication is given by Amanda or her parents that the child is worried that her mother is in any danger. In addition, Amanda is able to act appropriately, and without fear, when interacting with her church friends and her relatives. Therefore, the diagnosis of Separation Anxiety Disorder must be ruled out.

According to the DSM-IV, social phobia is to be diagnosed under the following conditions:

A. Excessive fear when the individual is exposed to a situation in which he or she will be observed or scrutinized by others; the individual believes he or she may be embarrassed

B. Confronting the feared situation almost always leads to anxiety; in the case of children, this anxiety may manifest itself as crying, freezing, tantrums, or shrinking from unfamiliar people

C. The individual is aware that the fear is excessive; however, children may not meet this criterion

D. The feared situation is avoided or endured with intense anxiety

E. Daily functioning is significantly disrupted

F. Duration of at least six months in children

G. Symptoms are not better accounted for by another disorder or a general medical condition and are not caused by the effects of a drug

H. If a general medical condition or disorder is present, the fear in condition A. is not related

Discussion

While Amanda's case should properly be diagnosed as Social Phobia, her mother's overinvolvement with her daughter and the strict rules that both parents have instituted seem relevant to Amanda's overall functioning. Therefore, it was determined that therapy would consist of weekly sessions with Amanda, weekly sessions with Amanda's parents, and monthly sessions with the family. The parents, at first resistant to being seen, were convinced that therapy could help them learn ways to help Amanda.

During the individual sessions with Amanda, the therapist began in a playroom. During the first week, Amanda spent the entire time playing with the Barbie doll she had brought with her. During subsequent sessions, Amanda was not allowed to bring any toys into the playroom with her. Starting with the second session, Amanda began to play more freely with the toys and developed a trusting relationship with the therapist. At this point, the therapist began using the dolls to stage common school and play scenes in which Amanda might find herself. On one occasion, Amanda and the therapist acted out a scene in which a child vomits in the middle of lunch. Amanda's doll immediately helped the sick doll and became her friend.

In the sessions with Amanda's parents, the therapist began exploring the rules in the house. It quickly became evident that both parents had been brought up with strict rules and considered themselves strict, but good, parents. The therapist steered discussion into how the strict rules they grew up with affected their peer interactions. At first, Amanda's father and then Amanda's mother began discussing how they felt different from their peers and how, at times, this had made their life very difficult. Over the course of the first month, both parents began to question whether they needed to be quite as strict with Amanda, especially as she was beginning to get older.

At the first family session, the therapist was pleased to see that although Amanda sat next to her mother, she was not sitting on her mother's lap. In addition, Amanda was wearing blue jeans and a t-shirt. Amanda proudly told the therapist she had made a new friend at school, Kristie, and that she had been invited over to Kristie's house. Mrs. Anderson reported that she was somewhat concerned about Amanda going to Kristie's house and had not yet given permission. At this point, the therapist asked under what conditions Mrs. Anderson might feel comfortable. After discussion, it was agreed that Mrs. Anderson would call Kristie's mother and take Amanda to Kristie's house. Amanda was quite pleased with these results and was willing to discuss other household rules. By the end of the first family session, the parents had agreed to allow Amanda to ride her bicycle in the street as long as she was with another child or an adult and wore her helmet. In addition, she would be allowed to play with two of the children in the neighborhood whose parents the Andersons knew and trusted.

Over the course of the next six months, therapy progressed slowly but well. After two months, the therapist was able to obtain permission from the Andersons to contact Amanda's teacher. Mrs. Osborne, Amanda's teacher, was pleased to learn Amanda had been seeing a therapist and reported that she had been quite concerned about Amanda based on the reports she had received from Amanda's kindergarten teacher. However, Mrs. Osborne only had to send Amanda home twice because of crying. On both occasions, Amanda had also shown some signs of illness such as an upset stomach, which allowed Mrs. Osborne to tell the other children Amanda was crying because her stomach hurt, not because she was a "crybaby." Both of these incidents occurred during the first month of school. Despite this, Mrs. Osborne had noticed that the other children seemed to tease Amanda more frequently than other children and that Amanda was more isolated than any other child. However, a new child, Kristie, had entered the school approximately ten weeks before. Amanda had immediately made friends with her when the other children held back. Since Kristie was fairly popular now, Amanda had received less teasing. Academically, Mrs. Osborne reported that, while Amanda would probably never be a straight-A student, she worked hard and was able to earn Bs in all subjects.

At six months, the parent sessions were terminated. The family sessions continued to be part negotiation and part monitoring of previous issues. Amanda's sessions continued to focus on modeling difficult situations.

At the end of eight months, both the parents and Amanda felt comfortable terminating therapy. While Amanda was still not allowed to listen to modern music, the rules in the family seemed more appropriate to Amanda and her parents. Even more important, Amanda was able to ride the school bus without significant anxiety or any somatic complaints. In addition, she and Kristie had successfully weathered three fights and were still best friends. Amanda reported that she still hated math but felt that recess and gym, at least, were fun.

CASE 9   *Ian*

Diagnosis: Selective Mutism

According to the DSM-IV, selective mutism is diagnosed when the individual had met the following five criteria:

   A. In situations in which the social expectation is for speaking, the individual repeatedly refuses to speak despite speaking in some situations
   B. Must be impairments in educational or occupational achievement, or with social communication
   C. Duration must be at least one month and not limited to the first month of school
   D. Failure to speak must not be caused by lack of knowledge of, or comfort with, the spoken language
   E. Disturbance is not better accounted for by another disorder such as a Communication Disorder (e.g., Stuttering); disturbance must also not be confined to the occurrence of a Pervasive Developmental Disorder, Schizophrenia, or other Psychotic Disorder

Discussion

Further testing seemed of little use in this case. Therefore, the school psychologist referred Ian and his parents to a local clinical psychologist.

The psychologist interviewed Ian's parents first. During this interview, the parents repeated much of the information given by them to the school psychologist. Based on the report of the school psychologist, the clinical psychologist asked about the camping trip of the past summer.

Ian and two friends had been taken camping by his friends' father, Mr. X. They had spent three nights at a park approximately one hour from Ian's home. Mr. X is a teacher at Ian's school and has been friends with Ian's parents for over five years.

At this point, the psychologist became concerned that Ian may have been abused during the camping trip by the father of the other two boys.

While the parents reported no change in Ian's behavior at home following the trip, Chris had indicated a change in Ian's behavior.

The psychologist indicated to Ian's parents that perhaps Ian had been frightened on the trip and had associated it with school because Mr. X was a teacher. While skeptical, Ian's parents were willing for the psychologist to talk with their neighbor.

When called, Mr. X had difficulty remembering the camping trip in question. Upon reflection, he was able to recall the trip and appeared willing to volunteer any information he could to help Ian. Mr. X reported that the trip was fairly uneventful. Ian had never gone camping before and needed extra help in setting up his tent and getting his sleeping bag organized. At the end of each day, they would sit around the fire and tell scary stories. Mr. X reported that on the third night he remembered telling a story that seemed to especially scare Ian. The story centered around a teacher who stalked and killed children at his school, sometimes putting poison in their lunches.

While questioning the judgment of Mr. X in telling Ian and his sons such stories, the therapist felt confident that Ian had not been physically or sexually abused. With this information in hand, the therapist scheduled a meeting with Ian's parents and his teacher. After explaining about the scary story, Ian's mother reported that she did not allow Ian to watch any scary shows because they frightened him.

Since selective mutism is typically a time limited disorder, several treatment strategies were agreed on by the parents, the teacher, and the therapist. First, a thorough physical evaluation was recommended to be conducted by Ian's pediatrician. At school, Ian would be encouraged and rewarded for talking to Chris. Ian would begin bringing his lunch from home and would be allowed to keep his lunch in his desk until lunchtime. In addition, Ian's teacher, with the help of the therapist, would begin a unit discussing feelings. It was agreed that the parents, teacher, and therapist would meet once a week to assess progress.

At the end of the first week, Ian continued to talk with Chris. Since he had been bringing his lunch, he now ate with the other children. No other changes were noted. The physical evaluation had been completed and Ian was pronounced healthy.

At the end of the second week, Ian's teacher was pleased to note that Ian was now willing to talk to one other child, Eric. By the third week, Ian continued to talk with Chris and Eric and was joining in activities during gym. At the end of four weeks, Ian's teacher excitedly reported that Ian was taking part in spelling and math quizzes during class.

Weekly progress continued with minor improvements each week in talking in the classroom and participating in class activities. The lunchroom continued to be a problem for several months. Eventually, the therapist and teacher took Ian on a tour of the lunchroom demonstrating how only the cooks had access to the food. One of the cooks allowed Ian to put cookies in the oven during the tour. That day, Ian ate one cookie from the lunch-room.

Three months later, Ian continued to be somewhat shy but was otherwise indistinguishable from his peers. While he brought his lunch on occasion, Ian usually ate his lunch in the lunchroom and had become friends with many of the cooks. Ian's parents reported to the therapist and teacher that Ian had mentioned that he wanted to go camping again in the summer but that this time he wouldn't believe Mr. X's stories.

CASE **10**   *Chelsea*

Diagnosis: Alcohol Dependence, with Physical Dependence

Chelsea presents with a prolonged pattern of alcohol use that has led to the use of increased amounts of alcohol, negative social consequences, and unsuccessful attempts to control her alcohol use. Her symptoms meet the criteria outlined by the DSM-IV for this diagnosis.

Three of the following criteria must be met over a twelve-month period, leading to clinically significant impairment or distress:

A. Tolerance, defined as:
   1. A need to increase the amount of the substance to achieve desired effects, or
   2. Diminished effect with use of the same amount
B. Withdrawal, defined as:
   1. Characteristic withdrawal syndrome outlined in the DSM-IV, including physical or perceptual symptoms following cessation of substance use, or
   2. The same (or a closely related) substance is used to relieve or avoid withdrawal symptoms
C. Substance taken in larger amounts over a longer period than intended
D. Persistent desire or unsuccessful efforts to stop use of the substance
E. Inordinate amount of time spent obtaining substance, using substance, or recovering from the effects of the substance
F. Important social, occupational, or recreational activities are given up or reduced because of substance use
G. Substance is used despite knowledge that substance has already caused or exacerbated harmful physical or psychological problems

Physiological Dependence must be diagnosed when tolerance or withdrawal are documented (Criterion A. or B.). In Chelsea's case, Criterion A., tolerance, was clearly documented necessitating the addition of this specifier.

Discussion

Chelsea was fortunate in that she had two strongly supportive parents who addressed her problems as a family issue. Chelsea's father immediately scheduled a family session with the therapist and asked about local chapters of Alcoholics Anonymous for his daughter. Through the university, Chelsea was able to attend AA meetings for adolescents and young adults. At first Chelsea attended AA twice a week. After three months of sobriety, Chelsea reduced her attendance to once a week. Unfortunately, Chelsea attended an end-of-school party with two of her friends and drank again. Chelsea was able to call her father after three drinks. After this incident, Chelsea decided to no longer attend parties on campus. With the help of the therapist, Chelsea was able to convince her parents to allow her to work at a local stable over the summer. In exchange for cleaning out the stalls, exercising the horses, and cleaning and feeding the horses, Chelsea was given free lessons and earned $100 a week. Her employer took an interest in Chelsea and got her involved in a local group of horse enthusiasts. At the end of six months, Chelsea was once again sober.

At the first family session, Chelsea spent twenty minutes outlining her escalating use of alcohol and her fears that she would not be able to stop drinking. Her parents also discussed their fears of Chelsea becoming an alcoholic like her grandmother and their own frustration at not recognizing the seriousness of Chelsea's problems.

Chelsea's mother, Mrs. Stanley, admitted that she had been concerned that Chelsea was drinking. She noted that she was hesitant to address the issue as she did not want to cause any arguments. Mrs. Stanley went on to describe how Chelsea had become more argumentative since she had reached adolescence.

Chelsea acknowledged that she and her mother seemed to fight frequently but felt that most of the problems were a result of her mother not being willing to allow Chelsea to make her own decisions. Mr. Stanley seemed confused by his wife's and daughter's comments, stating that he was unaware of the arguments between the two.

Over the next six months, the Stanleys met with the therapist on a weekly basis. One of the major issues for the family centered around Chelsea's need for increased independence. Getting Mrs. Stanley to agree to Chelsea's part-time job at the stable was a major struggle accomplished only with much negotiation on the part of the therapist. Once the decision had been reached, however, Mrs. Stanley was supportive of her daughter's decision, even buying her new boots. Mrs. Stanley and Chelsea improved their skills in this area with the aid of the therapist. Mr. Stanley was quite beneficial in this regard, developing the ability to reflect the concerns of his wife and daughter in a clear and concise manner.

A second issue that arose during therapy was the protection of Mr. Stanley by his wife and daughter. Problems in the family were handled without discussing them with Mr. Stanley. Repeatedly, Mr. Stanley expressed surprise as his wife and Chelsea expressed their concerns. Mrs. Stanley commented that since her husband worked, she believed it was her responsibility to handle the problems in the home and not "worry" her husband. Chelsea commented that, to her, it was "like walking on eggshells" around her father.

This second issue was never fully resolved. Chelsea made an agreement with her parents that she would discuss all of her concerns with both of her parents. She stated that she preferred this because she felt less anxious around her father when she wasn't keeping secrets from him. Chelsea also reported that she believed discussions became less "explosive" when her father was part of the conversation. Mrs. Stanley, however, continued to keep most of the household problems from her husband, preferring to deal with them on her own.

At the beginning of Chelsea's junior year of high school, Chelsea had not taken a drink in three months. She had developed two new friends through her activities with the horse enthusiasts' group she had joined. Her parents agreed to allow her to continue working at the stable during the school year as long as her grades did not fall below a B and that she did not drink any alcohol. Chelsea was happy with this arrangement.

Therapy was reduced to once a month at this time. Many of the sessions continued to focus on Chelsea's increased need for independence and her desire to include her father in decisions involving her life. Chelsea became quite proficient at enlisting her father's opinions. Although this alliance between Chelsea and her father concerned the therapist at first, it became apparent that Chelsea was not manipulating this relationship. Over the course of the following year, Chelsea did not attend any parties on campus and did not drink any alcohol. In addition to her increasing involvement with horses, Chelsea went through training and began working as a volunteer for the crisis center. Therapy was discontinued at the end of Chelsea's junior year of high school.

The therapist received an invitation to Chelsea's graduation from high school the following year. Enclosed in the invitation was a note from Chelsea stating that she was still sober and that she planned to go to a large state university in another state. No further contact was received from Chelsea or her family.

CASE 11   *Lee*

Diagnosis: Alcohol Intoxication
              Marijuana Intoxication

Rule Out: Alcohol Abuse

In this case, whether Lee suffers from Alcohol Intoxication or Alcohol Abuse is not clear. For a diagnosis of Alcohol Abuse, it must be documented that a maladaptive pattern of alcohol use leads to clinically significant impairment or distress as manifested by repeated failure to fulfill major role obligations, repeated use of alcohol in physically dangerous situations, repeated alcohol-related legal problems, or continued alcohol use despite social or interpersonal problems. In Lee's case, on the basis of the initial evaluation it is unclear whether he meets these criteria. His alcohol use is recurrent. He is experiencing a failure to fulfill a major role obligation by being suspended. Unfortunately there is insufficient information to be able to clearly justify a diagnosis of Alcohol Abuse even though it seems likely that such is the case. According to the DSM-IV, Lee meets the criteria for Intoxication:

A. Reversible substance-specific (alcohol and marijuana, in Lee's case) syndrome, caused by recent ingestion or exposure to a substance

B. Clinically significant maladaptive behavioral or psychological changes directly a result of the substance's effect on the central nervous system, developing shortly after the use of the substance

C. During, or following, use of the substance, one or more of the following symptoms develop:
   1. Slurring of speech
   2. Lack of coordination
   3. Unsteady gait
   4. Decreases in memory or attention
   5. Rhythmic movements of the eye (nystagmus)

D. Symptoms must not be due to a general medical condition or another mental disorder

Discussion

Lee met with the school psychologist the following week. As dictated by school policy, Lee's locker had been searched each morning. No alcohol or other drugs were discovered. Lee entered the psychologist's office loudly, dropping his book bag onto the floor and kicking the door shut. Lee then slouched in the chair with one leg hanging over the arm and tapped out music with his fingers on his knees.

Despite repeated attempts to engage Lee in conversation, Lee continued to tap out his music and refused to directly look at or speak to the psychologist. At the end of the appointed time, Lee rose and left the room.

The psychologist called Lee's home and spoke with Mrs. Stratton. Though sympathetic, she answered the psychologist's questions evasively and finished by stating that the psychologist would have to talk with her husband. Mr. Stratton did not return the psychologist's calls.

The following week, Lee repeated his behavior of the previous week. When the psychologist informed Lee that the terms of their agreement dictated that Lee participate in treatment, Lee grinned and replied that he and his parents had only agreed to Lee attending sessions, not talking.

Once Lee had left, the psychologist discussed the situation with the headmaster. The headmaster decided that since no additional alcohol or marijuana had been found in Lee's locker and that Lee was resistant to therapy, the sessions should be discontinued. The headmaster informed the psychologist that he would call the Strattons and express his pleasure in Lee's improved behavior at school and his decision to discontinue therapy as long as no additional drugs were found in Lee's locker. Despite the protests of the psychologist, therapy was discontinued. At the end of two months, locker searches were discontinued.

The following year Lee was a passenger in a car accident. The driver, a sixteen-year-old student on the football team at the same school, was drunk and hit a tree. Lee and two other students were also drunk. All four were killed instantly.

This case was especially troubling because the parents of the four dead students reported that they were unaware of the danger of their children's alcohol use. Mrs. Stratton stated that she felt all teenagers drank a little and didn't know they would drive while drinking.

CASE 12   *Cathy*

Diagnosis: Paranoid Schizophrenia

Schizophrenia is only diagnosed when at least two of the following symptoms, present for at least a one-month period, are found:

   A. Delusions
   B. Hallucinations
   C. Disorganized speech
   D. Extremely disorganized or catatonic behavior, or
   E. So-called negative symptoms such as flattening of affect, alogia, or avolition

In addition, significant impairment in work, interpersonal relations, or self-care must be demonstrated. Continuous signs of these problems must occur over a six month period. Finally, other disorders such as Schizoaffective and Mood disorders must be ruled out as well as symptoms arising as a direct result of a substance or a general medical condition.

The DSM-IV lists Paranoid Schizophrenia as a type of Schizophrenia in which two criteria must be met:

   A. Individual must be preoccupied with one or more delusions, or frequent auditory hallucinations
   B. None of the following symptoms can be prominent: disorganized speech, disorganized or catatonic behavior, or flat or inappropriate affect

Discussion

At the end of the initial interviews with Cathy and her family, it seemed apparent that there were several interrelated problems. First, Cathy was exhibiting signs of a serious thought disorder. Specifically, she was demonstrating the illogical thinking, paranoia, auditory hallucinations, and delusions commonly seen in paranoid schizophrenia. Although Cathy had made a serious suicide attempt, it was felt that this suicide attempt was best understood as a result of her delusion rather than major depression.

In addition to the individual problems that Cathy presented, several family issues seemed to be relevant to Cathy's presenting complaint. Although three children were members of this family, it appeared that alliances had been made between Shelly and her father and between Aaron and his mother. Cathy did not seem to be aligned with anyone. Although the initial interview did not present sufficient information to be certain, the clinician was seriously concerned as to whether these alliances were particularly healthy. The father's descriptions of his daughter Shelly as "just darned cute" and his interactions with this daughter raised the possibility of an enmeshed relationship between the two or even a situation in which Shelly might begin to be perceived as more of a girlfriend than a daughter. The situation between Aaron and his mother was also of concern to the clinician. While breastfeeding is perfectly natural, and especially healthy for both the mother and the child, it appeared unusual for a mother to be breastfeeding a four-year-old. Of course, this situation may not have been of clinical significance. However, given the alliances seen in this family, the breastfeeding incident seemed worthy of future investigation.

Given these concerns, a three-pronged approach to treatment was devised. First, Cathy was referred to a psychiatrist for prescription and monitoring of antipsychotic medication. In addition, once medication had time to reduce some of Cathy's more active symptoms (i.e., her hallucinations, delusions, and illogical thinking), Cathy was seen by another clinician in individual therapy. The focus of this therapy was to help Cathy develop a more structured environment for herself and to allow her a safe haven for discussing any issues that might arise. Finally, the original clinician met with the entire family, including Cathy, for family therapy. Although the original clinician could have seen Cathy for both individual and family counseling, given the alliances already present in this family, it was felt that creating an additional alliance between Cathy and the therapist might sabotage improvement.

Cathy responded positively to the medication with a drastic decrease in hallucinations, delusions, and illogical thinking. She continued to be isolated, have trouble planning activities, and difficulty expressing her emotions. With the help of her individual clinician, Cathy was able to develop and adhere to a fairly structured daily routine. Her greatest difficulties occurred during weekends and school holidays.

Family therapy did not prove as successful. Shelly began complaining from the first family session. She indicated quite clearly that Cathy was the problem and the family was "perfectly okay." Interestingly, Cathy's father insisted that the family continue in family therapy because he believed they all could improve. Over the first several family sessions, the father was quite charming to the clinician and seemed very concerned with ensuring the success of therapy. Around the fourth week of family therapy, Cathy began to show marked decreases in her hallucinations, delusions, and illogical thinking. With this realization, Shelly became more vocal in her complaints about Cathy, Aaron, her mother, and, eventually, her father. At the fifth session, Shelly stated that she wanted the clinician to "fix a few things" for her. First, Shelly stated that she wanted her mother to stop sleeping in the same bed as Aaron because that meant her father frequently slept in Shelly and Cathy's room. Shelly then went on to report that she was tired of her father coming into the bathroom when she was showering and drying her with the towel once she finished. As Shelly finished talking, her father jumped to his feet and began yelling that he was going to South America and that she'd be glad to see him when he returned. Despite any attempt on the part of the clinician, the father then left the room. After he was gone, Shelly remained defiant, stating that none of her friends had to endure a father touching their breasts. When questioned about these incidents, Shelly's mother stated that as long as her husband left her alone, she didn't really mind what he did. The mother went on to report that she hadn't slept in the same bed with her husband since Aaron was born and had no intentions of allowing him back into her bed. During this discussion, Cathy sat in her chair without saying a word.

The clinician discussed programs offered by the local child welfare agencies and informed the mother that the clinician would be contacting them. The mother seemed unconcerned about this development. Shelly, however, seemed quite concerned, saying that if her father really left the family wouldn't have sufficient money. The session ended with a meeting scheduled for the following week and a call to child welfare. At midweek, the clinician received a call from child welfare indicating that Shelly and the mother had denied any misbehavior on the part of the father. The day of the scheduled session, the mother telephoned the clinician to cancel the session, indicating that the father was out of the country and they were unsure when he would be returning. She indicated that her husband had refused to return for therapy, claiming that "all the attention gave the girls ideas." Cathy, fortunately, was allowed to continue with her clinician and her psychiatrist. Cathy was hospitalized again after about six months. Following this hospitalization, Cathy was placed in a group home for adolescents with serious psychological conditions. Cathy remained in this home for the following two years with no recurrence of psychotic symptoms. No further contact was possible after this point.

CASE 13   *Anne*

Diagnosis: Major Depressive Disorder

Rule Out: Borderline Personality Disorder

Anne is not unlike many children and adolescents whose symptoms may suggest more than one disorder. Whereas Anne's cult involvement may appear to be a red flag and the focus of her problems, the underlying low self-esteem and depressive symptomatology must be addressed. Anne's diagnosis reflects the seriousness of these underlying symptoms. This diagnosis must be made due to Anne's psychomotor agitation, difficulty sleeping, loss of interest or pleasure in activities previously enjoyed, diminished ability to concentrate, unexplained weight loss, and failure in school. In addition, her self-mutilation and possible identity problems clearly suggest the need to rule out Borderline Personality Disorder in future therapy sessions.

According to the DSM-IV, Major Depressive Disorder is diagnosed when the following five criteria are met:

A. Five or more of the following symptoms must be present nearly every day for a period of two weeks, represent a change from previous functioning, and must include either 1 or 2 below:
   1. Depressed mood (can be irritable in children or adolescents)
   2. Loss of interest or pleasure in all or almost all activities
   3. Weight loss when not dieting or an increase or decrease in appetite
   4. Insomnia or hypersomnia
   5. Objectively observed psychomotor agitation or retardation
   6. Fatigue or loss of energy
   7. Feelings of worthlessness or excessive or inappropriate guilt
   8. Difficulty thinking or concentrating, indecisiveness
   9. Suicidal ideation, with or without a plan, suicide attempts
B. Symptoms must not meet criteria for a Mixed Episode

C. Symptoms must lead to clinically significant impairment or distress in social, occupational, or other important areas of functioning
D. Symptoms must not be directly caused by a general medical condition or by
   the direct physiological effects of a substance
E. Symptoms must not be better accounted for by bereavement

Discussion

After the initial session, Anne's mother, Ms. Newsome, was brought back into
the office. The therapist explained that Anne was suffering from depression.
The therapist went on to reassure Anne's mother that although Anne's behavior may have seemed bizarre, Anne was not crazy. However, the therapist
also stressed Anne's situation was very serious, and needed to be treated as
quickly and effectively as possible. On the basis of this discussion, it was
agreed that Anne would be seen weekly for cognitive-behavioral therapy. The
therapist explained to Ms. Newsome that continual assessment of Anne's
condition would be made to avoid missing any additional developments. Ms.
Newsome asked about prescribing an antidepressant for her daughter. This
option was discussed at length. Although some clinicians have used antidepressants with children and adolescents, this is still somewhat controversial
because these drugs were developed for and tested on adults. Following this
discussion, Ms. Newsome agreed to first attempting to treat her daughter
without the use of drugs.

A cognitive behavioral treatment program was developed to address
Anne's problem areas. The program involved fourteen twice-weekly sessions
that focused on teaching methods of relaxation, increasing pleasant events,
controlling irrational and negative thoughts, and increasing social skills and
conflict resolution skills. In addition, the therapist included critical discussions of various religions because of Anne's interest in Satanism.

As a result of continued assessment during the program, the therapist
was able to rule out Borderline Personality Disorder. Anne did not demonstrate the identity problems inherent in this personality disorder. By the end
of the third week of therapy, Anne had ceased her involvement in Satanism,
had cut her hair to one length and stopped dyeing it, removed her make-up,
and was no longer dressing in black. Over the course of the next four weeks,
Anne began to show more affective expression, more interest in school and
her friends, and was able to laugh about her self-mutilation.

At the end of the treatment program, Anne contracted with the therapist for twelve additional sessions to discuss her feelings about her parents'
divorce. These sessions continued to be structured around the original treatment plan but with more focus on helping Anne express her feelings about
negative events and find constructive ways of dealing with these emotions.

Following these additional twelve sessions, Anne and her mother were able to agree to therapy being discontinued. The therapist received an invitation to Anne's high school graduation three years later.

CASE 14   *Jacob*

Diagnosis: Major Depressive Disorder

The criteria for depression in children and adults are the same (see Case 13, Anne, for a review of these criteria) although certain symptoms are more commonly seen in children. Somatic complaints, social withdrawal, and irritability are particularly common in children, whereas delusions, hypersomnia, and psychomotor retardation are less common before puberty. Jacob clearly shows the social isolation so common in depressed children his age.

Discussion

One of the primary concerns of the therapist was Jacob's overconcern for his mother. In young children, symptoms of depression may signal more systemic problems in the family. Although cognitive-behavioral treatment was seen as the treatment of choice for Jacob, the therapist decided to include a parent component to this treatment. The therapist believed that if additional problems in the family were contributing to Jacob's depression, this extra component might allow these issues to be addressed.

Jacob was seen by the therapist for three months. During these three months, the therapist and Jacob used role-play to teach interpersonal and problem-solving skills. Cognitive restructuring was also used to help Jacob alter maladaptive cognitions. Finally, Jacob was taught self-monitoring skills to assess his level of pleasant events. Jacob responded favorably to treatment. His teacher reported that Jacob, although still shy, was interacting with the other children and contributing to class discussions.

Jacob's parents attended weekly sessions separate from Jacob. During these sessions, the Samuels received an overview of the techniques being taught to Jacob. Both of the Samuels expressed interest in learning these techniques to help themselves. As a result, the therapist began teaching some of the same skills to the Samuels as Jacob was learning. During the course of these sessions, Mrs. Samuels expressed relief at the effectiveness of these techniques and discussed her feelings of being overwhelmed by the children. With the aid of the therapist, Mrs. Samuels was able to express her feelings of being confined to the house and her desire to return to college. While initially opposed to this idea, Mr. Samuels came to encourage his wife. At the end of treatment, Mrs. Samuels had enrolled in two courses at a local community college. The children would be staying at their grandmother's house while she attended classes and studied.

Treatment was discontinued after three months for both Jacob and his parents. The therapist contacted the Samuels two years later as part of a research study on treatment effectiveness. Jacob reported no reoccurrence of symptoms of depression. Mrs. Samuels continued to take college classes and had decided to become a nurse.

CASE 15   *Carly*

Diagnosis: Major Depressive Disorder

Carly clearly meets the criteria for depression (see Case 13, Anne, for a review of these criteria). Her presentation is somewhat unusual in that she exhibits some of what have been called "vegetative" symptoms of depression including her recent weight gain. One of the most disturbing developments in Carly's case is her attempted suicide.

The attempted suicide motivated Carly's parents to view her problems very seriously. Up to this point, the Prochaskis had been somewhat concerned about her grades but confused. It is not uncommon for changes in school performance to be one of the first symptoms noted by parents. Prior to the interview with the therapist, the Prochaskis viewed their daughter as happy and healthy with no significant problems. When Carly took the bottle of aspirin, she changed her parents' attitude.

After speaking with Carly's mother, the interviewer called the psychologist at the hospital where Carly had been taken. The psychologist reported that Carly would be kept in the hospital for only seventy-two hours. Carly was denying that she had meant to kill herself. Carly had reported to the hospital psychologist that she had been experiencing menstrual cramps and had simply lost count of the number of aspirin she had taken. Although the hospital psychologist did not believe this report, Carly was not reporting any intent to harm herself or others at this point.

Based on assessment completed in the hospital, an antidepressant, imipramine, was prescribed for Carly. At discharge, Carly was scheduled for a follow-up appointment to see a psychiatrist for her medication and for an appointment with the original therapist.

On the morning of the scheduled appointment, Mrs. Prochaski called to postpone the appointment stating that Carly was in an excellent mood and no longer seemed depressed. Mrs. Prochaski reported that Carly had played several games of Scrabble with her parents the previous evening and had arranged a dinner party for several of her friends from school for that evening. An appointment was scheduled for the following week.

Two days later the therapist received a telephone call from Carly's father reporting that Carly had killed herself in the middle of the night. After her parents had gone to sleep, Carly had filled her tub with hot water, took all of her medication, and slit her wrists. Mrs. Prochaski had found her the following morning when she went to awaken her for church.

Cases such as Carly's are heartbreaking for all concerned. Not all depressed adolescents commit suicide but the risk is substantial. Although initially the Prochaskis did not recognize Carly's symptoms as depression, this is not unusual. They became very concerned once they recognized the problem and after Carly took the bottle of aspirin. Unfortunately, the Prochaskis were fooled by Carly's improved mood following her hospitalization. Seemingly, Carly had returned to normal. She was playing games of Scrabble with them and meeting with her friends. This improved mood misled them into believing Carly was significantly improved. It is not unusual to see individuals who have decided to kill themselves improve in mood. Some clinicians attribute this improved mood to a lessening of worry once the decision has finally been made to end their life. Other clinicians point out that improved mood accompanies an increase in energy. Prior to this, the depressed individuals may have wanted to kill themselves but did not have the energy to complete the task. Once they have improved a little, they have the energy to follow through on the desire to die.

The Prochaskis declined therapy to deal with their grief over the loss of Carly. The therapist noted that the Prochaskis divorced six months after Carly's death.

In a case such as this, little else could have been done to help Carly. Carly had only been on her medication a few days at the time of her death. Imipramine has been shown to be effective (Dulcan et al., 1995) in treating adolescent depression. However, it is unlikely that Carly had been on the medication long enough for her to experience any significant improvement. Therapy, both cognitive-behavioral and interpersonal, has also been found to be effective for treating adolescent depression (see Case 13, Anne). Unfortunately, therapy did not have a chance to begin. Could Carly have been kept in the hospital, perhaps involuntarily, until the medication had a chance to show demonstrable results? It is possible that Carly's parents could have been convinced to hospitalize their daughter in a private facility but there were no clear indications that Carly needed inpatient care.

CASE 16   *Michael*

Diagnosis: Gender Identity Disorder in Children

According to the DSM-IV, Gender Identity Disorder (GID) is to be diagnosed when four criteria are met:

    A. Strong and persistent identification with the opposite gender as manifested by four of the following:
       1. Repeatedly stating the desire to be, or insistence that he or she is, the opposite sex
       2. In boys, preference for cross-dressing or simulating the attire of females; in girls, insistence on wearing only stereotypical male clothing
       3. Cross-sex preference in make-believe play or persistent fantasies of being the opposite sex
       4. Intense desire to participate in games and pastimes of the opposite sex
       5. Strong preference for playmates of the opposite sex
    B. Persistent discomfort with his or her sex, or sense of inappropriateness in the gender role of that sex. In children, this may be manifested by:
       For Boys:
       1. Assertion that penis or testes are disgusting or will disappear
       2. Aversion to rough-and-tumble play
       3. Rejection of stereotypical male toys, games, and activities
       For Girls:
       1. Rejection of urination while sitting
       2. Assertion that she will grow a penis
       3. Assertion that she does not want breasts or will not menstruate
       4. Marked aversion toward normative feminine clothing
    C. Disturbance is not concurrent with a physical intersex condition
    D. Must lead to clinically significant distress or impairment in daily functioning

Discussion

Although it is certainly clear from the criteria listed in the DSM-IV and the case presentation that this child meets the criteria for Gender Identity Disorder, even applying this diagnosis has recently become the center of a heated controversy. Neisen (1992) has argued that diagnosing children with Gender Identity Disorder (GID) reflects an intolerance of allowing individuals to express their sexuality. Some researchers (see, for example, Reid, 1989) have documented a higher incidence of homosexuality and bisexuality in adulthood among boys who were diagnosed with Gender Identity Disorder in childhood. Given this relationship, some have argued that Gender Identity Disorder is simply how children appear who later self-identify as gay or lesbian. Haroian (1992) argues that the issue of GID and homosexuality should be considered two separate issues, because some children may demonstrate homosexual or bisexual tendencies as children, yet as adults present as heterosexual. This is different, she argues, from GID. GID children are more likely to be transsexual as adults. However, it is certainly possible that a child will self-identify as homosexual given society's more open discussion of homosexuality over transsexuality.

A separate argument has been made that GID children, especially boys, are being punished for failing to conform to society. Girls, on the other hand, may be encouraged to be tomboys. This double standard is seen by proponents of this argument as the major issue in the diagnosis of children with this disorder.

On the other side of the controversy, some researchers and therapists note the intense distress, cognitive dissonance, and peer rejection experienced by these children and argue that failure to provide intervention is unconscionable. At least one study (Rekers, 1975) has documented that children diagnosed with Gender Identity Disorder and treated for this condition can be successfully reintegrated with their peer groups.

If the therapist does decide to diagnose the child, additional controversy awaits. The decision to treat this disorder having been made, it is now necessary to decide which treatment is to be used. Two general treatment methods are popular in the literature. The first involves inpatient care with a highly structured approach including aversive conditioning. The second treatment involves an outpatient approach using a behavioral modification program tailored to the individual.

Inpatient treatment typically involves a graduated program of earning privileges by meeting treatment goals. Therefore, children earn privileges, such as wearing their own clothing rather than hospital pajamas, by adhering to treatment regimens. Failure to follow hospital rules results in loss of privileges. In some of these programs, sexual attraction to members of the same sex may be punished through electrical shocks. While these procedures have been demonstrated to be effective in some studies, there are two major points to be remembered. First, ethical concerns have arisen about some of these programs regarding whether the program crosses the line, traumatizing the child more than the consequences of the disorder itself. Second, GID is not the same as homosexuality. These types of treatments are not appropriate and should not be used indiscriminately.

In the present case, Michael was diagnosed with GID and the therapist decided on the second type of treatment involving outpatient treatment and a more individualized behavioral modification package. Michael was seen twice a week for the first month. During these sessions, the male therapist met Michael at the door to the therapist's office. During the first fifty-minute session the therapist and Michael talked as they walked around the neighborhood. During this session, much care was taken to develop a strong relationship between the therapist and Michael. The second session was also conducted outside. This time, the therapist walked to a local elementary school and shot baskets while he and Michael talked. For the first ten minutes, Michael refused to shoot the ball, but by the end of the session Michael began shooting the ball. During the third session, Michael was reinforced for any shot that was not made underhanded regardless of whether he made a basket. In addition, the therapist began selective responding to masculine or neutral topics. Feminine topics were ignored. Interestingly, this not only resulted in a decrease in feminine topics with a corresponding increase in masculine and neutral topics, but Michael also lost many of his feminine intonations including the giggling and high-pitched voice. At the fourth session, Michael's shirt came untucked when he jumped to make a shot. The therapist quickly encouraged Michael to leave his shirt untucked and commiserated with him when his long hair got in his eyes, pointing out how his own haircut was less trouble and stayed out of his way.

At the beginning of the fifth session, Mrs. Sunderson stated that she wished to speak with the therapist. Michael was asked to remain in the waiting room while the therapist talked with his mother. Once seated, Mrs. Sunderson expressed concern about the therapy sessions suggesting that perhaps it was time to stop therapy. She reported that Michael was becoming more like his father and even wanted to get his hair cut. When questioned by the therapist as to why these two developments were negative, the mother became flustered. The therapist used this opportunity to outline the advantages to Michael of developing friendships with other boys. In addition, the mother was offered counseling to help her adjust to the many demands she might have as a single mother. The therapist was concerned that Mrs. Sunderson might have unresolved issues from her divorce that might be impacting Michael's development. Directly confronting Mrs. Sunderson was not viewed as the most productive method of dealing with these issues because she might have responded by removing Michael from therapy. Mrs. Sunderson seemed to respond favorably to the therapist's acknowledgment of how difficult her life was and scheduled a session with a colleague of the therapist's. Mrs. Sunderson also agreed to a system of reinforcing Michael with tokens when he discussed masculine or neutral topics in the home. Finally, Mrs. Sunderson agreed to consider the possibility of allowing Michael to get his hair cut. She commented that she had seen a neighbor boy with an attractive haircut and wondered if Michael might like his hair cut in a similar manner.

Between the sixth and seventh session, Michael got his hair cut into a traditional boy's cut. Michael was very proud of his new haircut and explained to the therapist how he washed it each morning so he would look nice. Over the next several sessions, the therapist focused on reinforcing more stereotypical male patterns of sitting, walking, and talking. This process was facilitated by Michael's identification with the therapist. During the sixth week of therapy (twelfth session), Michael's teacher was recruited. At school, Michael would be given a certain number of points at the beginning of each day. He would lose points for engaging in behavior the teacher found problematic, such as crying and arguing with the other children by claiming that he would become a girl. Once these behaviors had decreased, additional behaviors were targeted such as giggling, crossing his legs in a feminine manner, and other feminine behaviors.

After the third month of treatment, a local Big Brothers Group was contacted and Michael was supplied with a Big Brother who was willing to work with Michael and the therapist. Michael was assigned a man who was also a police officer. This man worked with the therapist and served as a masculine role model for Michael.

During the time that Michael was being seen by the therapist, Mrs. Sunderson was being seen by her own therapist. As Michael's therapist had suspected, Mrs. Sunderson was very angry with her ex-husband for leaving her and returning to Sweden. Her anger encompassed not just her husband, but all men. As Mrs. Sunderson and her therapist worked on these issues, Mrs. Sunderson became more comfortable with Michael showing more masculine behavior ". . . like his father."

Fifteen months into treatment, Michael's "big brother" married Michael's mother. This development allowed Michael to move to a new school. The children in his new school were unaware of Michael's previous difficulties and accepted him readily. Michael joined the choir and ran cross-country. Therapy was discontinued at this time.

The therapist contacted the family five years later when Michael was in the eighth grade. Michael was continuing to be well-accepted by his peers, continued to run cross-country, and had become heavily involved in community theater. His stepfather and mother encouraged his varied interests and reported no significant problems.

CASE 17 *Elizabeth*

Diagnosis: Bulimia Nervosa, Purging Type
             Major Depressive Disorder

Although the primary focus of Elizabeth's disorder seems to be Bulimia Nervosa (i.e., her ongoing and increasing preoccupation with food, binge eating, and subsequent vomiting), the presence of overt depressive symptoms cannot be ignored. Elizabeth exhibits clear indications of depression in her loss of interest and pleasure in friends and activities, social isolation, self-mutilation, slow affect, difficulty concentrating, and suicidal ideation (See Case 13, Anne, for a complete listing of DSM-IV criteria for depression). The comorbidity of bulimia nervosa and depression is a consistent finding both clinically and empirically and will be discussed in more detail in the discussion below.

According to the DSM-IV, the diagnosis of Bulimia Nervosa is made when the following criteria are met:

A. Repeated episodes of binge eating that include:
   1. Eating, in a circumscribed time period, of larger quantities of food than most people eat
   2. Individual experiences a subjective sense of loss of control over eating
B. Repeated behavior to attempt to compensate for the binge eating and avoid weight gain that typically includes self-induced vomiting; misuse of laxatives, diuretics, enemas, or other medications; fasting; or excessive exercise
C. Behaviors described in A and B both occur, on average, at least twice a week for three months
D. Self-evaluation highly influenced by body shape and size
E. Disturbance does not occur exclusively during episodes of Anorexia Nervosa

Purging type is specified in this case because Elizabeth regularly engaged in self-induced vomiting. The Nonpurging type specifier is only used in those cases in which the individual uses other compensatory behavior such as fasting or excessive exercise.

Discussion

Based on Elizabeth's presentation, the therapist decided to attempt cognitive-behavioral therapy on an outpatient basis. Elizabeth's condition was serious but not so serious that hospitalization was required. A contract was made in which Elizabeth agreed to see the therapist twice a week for at least twelve sessions. Elizabeth also agreed to call the therapist if she felt suicidal and agreed to self-monitor everything she ate, when she ate, her feelings when she ate, and all episodes of vomiting.

At the first session, Elizabeth had completed her self-monitoring sheets fairly well. Therapy focused on addressing the thoughts and feelings preceding her binges and her vomiting. Techniques for increasing problem-solving skills and altering maladaptive cognitions were taught and practiced.

Three days after the first session, Elizabeth had a major binge in which she ate two Big Macs, three large orders of fries, a half-gallon of ice cream, and two packages of Hostess cupcakes. Following this binge, she attempted to vomit but could not. Elizabeth became so depressed that she decided to kill herself. After consuming three-fourths of a bottle of aspirin, she called the therapist. The therapist kept Elizabeth on the telephone while an ambulance was sent to take her to the hospital.

At this point the decision was made to hospitalize Elizabeth. Once Elizabeth had recovered from her overdose, she was transferred from the general medical ward to the psychiatric unit. The hospital did not have a special ward for eating disorders. In the hospital, a multicomponent approach was taken to address Elizabeth's problems. A nutritionist was assigned to work with Elizabeth on creating a healthy diet, the therapist continued with cognitive behavioral treatment, and a psychiatrist prescribed medication. The use of an antidepressant was seen as a temporary measure to try to "break through" Elizabeth's depression and enable the cognitive behavioral treatment to work more effectively. Elizabeth was first given imipramine, then fluoxetine, and, finally, trazodone. Unfortunately, Elizabeth did not respond well to the antidepressants. At first she developed negative side effects including insomnia, nausea, and tremor. After the first two antidepressants, the nurses caught Elizabeth hoarding the third antidepressant. Elizabeth admitted that she was going to save enough to kill herself. As a result of these comments and previous unsuccessful use of antidepressants, no further antidepressants were tried.

Over the course of the following month, Elizabeth received individual cognitive behavioral therapy and nutritional counseling. Elizabeth also attended a group therapy session held in the hospital. This group consisted of adolescents with a variety of diagnoses but who all shared symptoms of depression. This group contact allowed Elizabeth to practice some of the interpersonal and problem-solving skills being learned in therapy.

Elizabeth was released from the hospital after eight weeks. At discharge she continued to experience negative thoughts about her size and to compare herself with other girls. Her binges and vomiting had disappeared. Elizabeth was sleeping better, was more interested in everyday activities, and was anxious to see her friends. No suicidal ideation was reported. Outpatient treatment was instituted on a weekly basis. Over the next six months of outpatient care, Elizabeth continued to express dissatisfaction with her weight and appearance. Since she did not report any binging or purging during this time, a light exercise program was developed for Elizabeth. This program consisted of daily walks and swimming twice a week.

At the end of six months, Elizabeth had lost twenty pounds without purging. She reported that on Friday nights she sometimes binged on pizza with her friends. When she did this, she walked thirty extra minutes the next day.

Therapy was discontinued by Elizabeth at this point. The therapist had some concerns about Elizabeth's ability to successfully navigate the change from high school to college without resorting to her binging and purging. It was agreed that Elizabeth would seek out a therapist at the student mental health center at her college if she experienced any urges to binge or purge.

One year later, the therapist received a call from a therapist at Elizabeth's college. This therapist reported that Elizabeth had come to the clinic following a binge episode. Elizabeth was able to work with the new therapist successfully, preventing any further binges. No purging or depressive symptoms were noted.

Maria

Diagnosis: Psychological Factors Affecting Medical Condition
             Maladaptive Health Behaviors Affecting Heart
             Functioning

The International Classification of Diseases, 10th edition (ICD-10) recognizes obesity as a general medical condition. Obesity does not appear in the DSM-IV (1994) because it has not been empirically established that obesity is consistently associated with a psychological or behavioral syndrome.

In the present case, Maria has been advised to lose weight because of her physician's concern about the effect of the excess weight on her heart. Since Maria's heart was damaged by her bout with rheumatic fever, the physician's concern appears highly justified. According to the DSM-IV, the category Psychological Factors Affecting Medical Condition should be utilized when the presence of one or more psychological or behavioral factors may adversely affect a general medical condition. Specifically, Maladaptive Health Behaviors specifier is chosen due to Maria's overeating and sedentary lifestyle being the focus of concern.

Discussion

Maria came to the first session in a subdued mood. After weighing in at 308 pounds, she reported that she desperately wanted to lose weight. She handed the therapist self-monitoring sheets that she had been keeping for the previous week. Although Maria had been taught self-monitoring during her previous treatment experience, the therapist was surprised that Maria had initiated this procedure on her own and viewed it as a positive predictor of treatment success. Maria reported that she was currently fourteen and in the eighth grade at her local junior high and was earning mainly Bs and Cs. Maria reported that the other children frequently called her names but that she had two good friends.

After a review of the previous treatment failure with Maria, a three-pronged approach to treatment was devised with her assistance. First, improving the nutritional quality and reducing Maria's caloric intake would be addressed through behavior modification procedures. Second, an exercise program consisting of walking would be devised. Third, Maria's school was contacted. At the school, the therapist was able to work with the school psychologist to develop a group for overweight students. The school psychologist ran this group with the aid of the therapist.

For the first component, a nutritionist was invited to therapy sessions with the therapist and Maria. During these three sessions, the nutritionist outlined a low-fat, low-cholesterol eating plan for Maria. Maria was allowed 1,500 calories a day. This contrasted sharply with Maria's self-monitoring sheets of what she had been eating prior to the beginning of treatment. Her sheets indicated that in an average day, Maria consumed between 5,000 and 6,000 calories. One of the most difficult aspects of this program for Maria was the absence of fast food. Given her love of fast food, two items were selected off the menus of each fast food establishment Maria and her friends frequented. For example, Maria frequented McDonald's almost every Friday night with her friends. It was agreed that Maria could eat a regular hamburger and drink diet cola. This compromise was acceptable to the nutritionist and made Maria happy.

Following the sessions with the nutritionist, the therapist focused on highlighting cues for eating based on Maria's self-monitoring sheets. The exercise portion of Maria's treatment was also devised and implemented. Maria was hesitant to begin any exercise regimen because she was concerned about her heart. After discussion with her physician, Maria was amenable to a walking program. A chart was developed for Maria to record how far she walked each day. Over the course of six weeks, Maria increased her daily walks until she was walking 1 mile each day.

With the involvement of the school psychologist, Maria's school developed a weight reduction group. Forty-five of the 300 students in the junior high joined the first group. These students met daily after school for exercise class. This one-hour class allowed students to choose between walking around the gym, an aerobics class, or shooting baskets. The last thirty minutes of the class was devoted to group discussions of problem areas and successes. The school administration was impressed with the effort of the students and added a salad and baked potato bar as an option to the traditional school lunch. In addition, the school developed a reward system based on students' achieving their weight loss goals. Students received rewards for each 10 pounds lost toward their goal and a large award for achieving their goal. Finally, the school discontinued their program of providing coupons to local fast-food restaurants as a reward for perfect attendance and honor roll. Instead, the school provided discount coupons for athletic events and amusement parks.

After the first week, Maria recorded a weight loss of four pounds. This was seen as a major accomplishment for Maria. The therapist praised Maria but cautioned her about how difficult the second week of changing habits could be. At the second session, Maria reported that she had eaten an ice cream cone at her grandmother's house. She noted that she was so upset she almost gave up but that she remembered the therapist had told her that such "slips" were okay. Maria was able to maintain her diet the rest of the week and weighed in with a 2-pound loss for the week. This was especially reassuring to Maria because she could see that one slip wouldn't destroy her diet. Over succeeding weeks, Maria continued to lose 2–3 pounds a week. At the end of twelve weeks, Maria had lost 30 pounds. When Maria came to this session she was quite excited because her mother had taken her to the mall the previous night and bought her a pair of blue jeans. This was the first time Maria had been bought blue jeans at the mall.

Over the course of the next twelve weeks, Maria lost another 25 pounds, bringing her weight down to 253 pounds. At this point, Maria began to experience some reluctance to complete her self-monitoring sheets. In addition, she reported two major slips in one week involving ice cream and cookies. Maria was able to describe these incidents to her school weight reduction group who encouraged her to buy fat-free ice cream and cookies, so that if she slipped the consequences wouldn't be so bad. They also encouraged her to "make a deal" with her therapist that as long as she continued to lose weight, she wouldn't have to fill out the self-monitoring sheets. Maria presented her case to the therapist. The therapist agreed to these conditions. Over the course of the following twelve weeks, Maria lost between 2 and 3 pounds each week, leading to a weight of 224 pounds.

At this point, the therapist and Maria agreed to monthly meetings rather than weekly sessions. As Maria came nearer to her goal weight, it was felt that the structure of therapy needed to be reduced. School would be dismissing for the summer within two months, leading to a discontinuation of the weight reduction group. The therapist was concerned about Maria losing both sources of support.

At the first monthly session, Maria had lost 8 pounds. The second monthly session was also successful, with a weight loss of 10 pounds. The therapist and Maria discussed school ending and Maria reported that the weight reduction group had decided to meet once a week over the summer. Interestingly, although no treatment had been aimed at improving Maria's performance in school, her grades at the end of the year had improved to all As, with a single B in math. Maria reported that she felt happier at school and that made studying easier.

Over the summer Maria continued to lose between 8 and 12 pounds a month. In addition to walking a mile each day, Maria enrolled in a swimming class with a friend. She went to the pool three to four times a week after completing the class. Upon entering the ninth grade, Maria weighed 175 pounds. From September to December, Maria met with the therapist twice. After the

Christmas holidays, Maria met with the therapist for the last time. At weigh-in, Maria weighed 150 pounds. This weight was acceptable to Maria's physician, her mother, and Maria. In June, Maria called the therapist to let her know that her weight continued to hover between 145 and 155 and that she had finally earned an A in math. The therapist received no further contact from Maria.

CASE 19 *Lisa*

Diagnosis: Anorexia Nervosa, Restricting Type

According to the DSM-IV, Anorexia Nervosa is to be diagnosed when four criteria are met:

A. There must be a refusal to maintain normal body weight for the individual's height and age. The cutoff is suggested at failure to maintain 85 percent of that expected

B. The individual must display an intense fear of gaining weight or becoming "fat," even though the person is obviously underweight

C. The person has a "disturbed body image;" the individual may show this disturbance in terms of evaluation of weight, shape, or denial of the seriousness of the weight loss

D. In postmenarchal women, the absence of three consecutive menstrual periods not due to pregnancy

In Lisa's case, Restricting Type would be diagnosed because of the absence of binge-eating or purging behavior.

Discussion

While still functioning very well, Lisa demonstrates classic signs of anorexia nervosa, including the weight loss, distorted body image, cessation of menstruation, obsession with food, and excessive exercise. The therapist felt Lisa had lost sufficient weight to necessitate medical intervention.

After a lengthy discussion with Lisa's parents, Lisa was taken to her family physician for a thorough evaluation. Fortunately, the physician was quite alarmed by Lisa's weight loss and possible negative effects on her body. The physician and the therapist, working together, were able to convince Mr. and Mrs. Baker of the seriousness of Lisa's condition.

Lisa was removed from college for the spring semester. Lisa began seeing the therapist on an outpatient basis and her parents met with a separate therapist. However, Lisa's condition continued to deteriorate, and by February she was down to 75 pounds. At this point, a decision was made to hospitalize Lisa in an attempt to stabilize her. Lisa was also seen by a nutritionist and a psychiatrist.

Over the course of her three-week hospitalization, Lisa became more and more depressed, necessitating the administration of antidepressant medication. This seemed to help Lisa. Her depression lifted and she was willing to work with the nutritionist and the therapist. Lisa was released from the hospital once she was voluntarily eating two meals a day. While these meals were small (one-half of an apple for breakfast, one-half of a piece of fish and a spoon of green beans for dinner), Lisa had eaten these meals freely.

As an outpatient, Lisa met weekly with her individual therapist and her nutritionist. Her individual therapist focused on cognitive-behavioral issues relating to self-esteem, control, and independence. In addition, Lisa and her parents met with a family therapist every two weeks. Finally, Lisa met with her psychiatrist once a month for the monitoring of her medication. At the end of three months, Lisa was taken off the antidepressants.

By the end of May, Lisa weighed 100 pounds and was looking forward to returning to school in the fall. While several issues were still unresolved, including her distorted body image and her feelings of being unable to live up to her parents' expectations, Lisa was eating three meals a day. In addition, Lisa had changed her major to pre-med.

Once back at school, Lisa continued to see a therapist on campus. Lisa was able to maintain her body weight between 100–105 lbs. throughout the fall semester. While home over Thanksgiving, she relapsed for three days but was able to return to her normal eating patterns when she returned to school. This pattern of relapsing when she went home continued throughout her college career. Lisa terminated therapy when she was accepted into a medical school on the West Coast. At the time she left therapy, Lisa weighed 105 pounds.

Patrick

Diagnosis: Sleep Terror Disorder
             Sleepwalking Disorder

Patrick's case is fairly straightforward in terms of the presentation of his symptoms. His recurrent and pervasive episodes of abrupt awakening from sleep with bloodcurdling screams, accompanied by amnesia, is a classic presentation of sleep terrors. The amnesia for the event effectively eliminates Nightmare Disorder from consideration. According to the DSM-IV, in order to diagnose an individual as suffering from Sleep Terror Disorder, five conditions must be met:

A. Repeated episodes of abrupt awakenings from sleep, usually beginning with a panicky scream

B. Intense fear and signs of autonomic arousal including tachycardia, rapid breathing, and sweating

C. Unresponsive to others' attempts at comforting

D. Amnesia for the episode including absence of recalled dream

E. Demonstrated clinically significant distress or impairment in social, occupational, or other important areas of functioning

In Patrick's case an additional diagnosis of Sleepwalking Disorder is also warranted. According to the DSM-IV, six (6) additional criteria are required for this disorder:

A. Repeated episodes of rising from bed during sleep and walking about

B. During these episodes, the individual has a blank, staring face and is unresponsive to others

C. Upon awakening, the individual has amnesia for the event

D. Shortly after the event, the individual has no impairment of mental activity or behavior

E. Clinically significant distress or impairment in functioning is demonstrated

F. Disturbance is not due to the direct physiological effects of a substance or a general medical condition

Discussion

Patrick's night terror episodes increase dramatically during Little League. Patrick, himself, seemed to be able to acknowledge the pressure he felt to perform well in baseball. Patrick's parents, however, did not appear to associate their son's playing baseball with the increase in his night terrors.

In the opinion of the therapist, the relationship between Little League and his night terrors was too strong to ignore. Patrick did not wish to be taken out of Little League, he simply wanted less pressure. Following discussion with Patrick, the therapist met with Patrick's parents. Very carefully, the therapist described Patrick's love of sports, especially baseball. The therapist also stressed how grateful Patrick was to his parents for all the help they gave him in baseball. The therapist then suggested that Patrick might, while sleeping, become anxious about doing well in baseball, causing the episodes the Callahans had been experiencing. Both of the Callahans were initially resistant to this linking of the night terrors with baseball but were able to accept that this was happening while Patrick was asleep, and therefore wasn't in control of these thoughts.

Following this explanation, the Callahans agreed to attend only Patrick's games and not his practices. In addition, the Callahans were not allowed to discuss Patrick's performance with him other than to tell him he had done a great job. Since the Callahans knew the coach quite well, it was agreed that any suggestions they had could be relayed to the coach. Finally, after each game the Callahans would take Patrick out to eat. This treat would occur regardless of whether Patrick's team won or lost. This last rule was hotly debated as Mr. Callahan initially believed that the therapist was suggesting that Patrick be rewarded for playing poorly. The therapist was able to change this impression by having Mr. Callahan talk about his own days on the baseball team and how sometimes he played very well but his team might still lose the game. Going out to eat would be a reward for playing hard and to let Patrick know how proud his parents were of him. Both of the Callahans were accepting of this.

Mrs. Callahan reported that she had read in a magazine that drinking milk and eating cookies before bedtime could improve sleeping. The therapist explained that milk contained a substance that could improve sleep and that there was no harm in trying this technique too. The therapist stressed, however, that one hour before bedtime should be free of arguments or discussions of sports.

The Callahans agreed to meet with the therapist for four weekly sessions to attempt the suggestions made by the therapist. At the first session, the Callahans reported that Patrick had experienced only one episode since the last session and this was following a practice where Mr. Callahan had stayed to watch his son. Mr. Callahan agreed not to attend any future practices although he was skeptical about the relationship between his attendance and the occurrence of the episode.

At the second and third session, Patrick had experienced no episodes of night terrors or of sleepwalking. Patrick reported that he was having a great season in baseball and enjoyed his parents coming only to his games. He told his parents that he used to be worried about "messing up" in practice but now he felt that the coach could help him fix any problems he had. He noted that the coach seemed to be helping him much more. Mr. Callahan was pleased with this report as he felt that his comments to the coach were leading to his son getting better coaching.

At the fourth session, Patrick continued to have no reported episodes of sleepwalking or night terrors. Mrs. Callahan reported that she missed seeing Patrick practice but that now she had more time to do things that she needed to do or for her and her husband to do things together. It was agreed that the Callahans would meet with the therapist in one month.

At the one month meeting, Patrick had experienced one episode of sleepwalking but no additional night terror episodes. The sleepwalking occurred the night of his first game. The Callahans agreed to call the therapist if Patrick's episodes reoccurred. One year later, the therapist received a call from Mrs. Callahan reporting that Patrick experienced an occasional sleepwalking episode (once every two to three months) but that his night terrors had completely disappeared. She questioned whether she and her husband had been "putting too much pressure" on Patrick about sports. The therapist noted that while that was always a possibility, Patrick appeared to be thriving now and for the Callahans to continue their current style of interacting with their son. No further contact was made with the therapist by the Callahans.

CASE 21   *Joe and Erin*

Diagnosis: Physical Abuse of Child

This condition may be found under the V Codes for Problems Related to Abuse or Neglect. According to the DSM-IV, this diagnosis should be used when treatment revolves around issues arising from the physical abuse of a child. Special codes are used to indicate whether the focus of treatment is on an adult who has been abused or a child who has been abused (995.5).

Discussion

According to Jones (1987), it is likely that certain families may not benefit from treatment. In particular, families who persist in denying the abuse, refuse to accept help, exhibit severe personality or psychiatric problems, and have a history of severe abuse are unlikely to benefit from treatment. In the present case, Mr. Hunter has acknowledged his abuse of his children and has directly asked for help. No evidence of serious personality or psychiatric problems was noted in the interviews with the children or their parents. Although the intensity of the physical abuse was increasing, the therapist believed that this family was capable of making significant progress.

Once Mrs. Hunter overcame her initial shock at her husband's admission, she became quite angry with him and expressed considerable self-blame for leaving her children with him while she worked. The parents were referred to a group counseling session for parents of abused children. This group consisted of both abusers and the nonabusing spouse. The focus of the group sessions was on anger management, dealing with self-blame, and parent effectiveness training. For the first month, Mrs. Hunter contemplated divorcing her husband. As she saw his struggles to change his responses, she decided that they could make their marriage work.

Joe and Erin continued to be seen by the therapist who had completed the initial interview. The court agreed to pay for this treatment because the relationship between the children and the therapist was seen as an important variable for treatment success. A majority of the research literature that focuses on treating children who have been physically abused (e.g., Seinfeld, 1989) highlights the importance of a strong empathic relatedness between the child and the therapist. This relationship allows the child to develop boundaries and to initiate therapeutic contact with the therapist. One of the most important goals of early therapy with such children is to create a safe "holding" environment for the child, allowing the child the security to explore more difficult issues.

Since Joe and Erin had developed a good relationship with the therapist, more difficult issues were broached. Separate sessions were continued for Joe and Erin because each child had different concerns. For Joe, anger was becoming a serious issue. When frustrated, Joe frequently responded in an aggressive manner (kicking a wall, stomping his feet) rather than talking through whatever had frustrated him. Given this issue, Joe and the therapist worked on problem-solving strategies. Erin's concerns included lower self-esteem and self-blame. Erin continued to believe that if she had "just been a better girl," her father would not have punished her. The therapist worked with Erin on cognitive restructuring through role-play and through play with the Barbie dolls.

Therapy continued for six months. During the second week of summer break, with the approval of the court, Mr. Hunter was allowed to return to his home. Prior to his reentry to the home, a series of five family sessions were held with the children's therapist and the parents' therapist. Joe and Erin were encouraged to express their feelings about the abuse to their father. Joe was able to accomplish this in a calm manner. Erin was reluctant to attempt this but, with encouragement from the therapist and Joe, was able to tell her father that he shouldn't have hurt her no matter what she did. This session was very emotional for the father as well. Mr. Hunter accepted full responsibility for his actions and apologized to his children and his wife.

Over the course of the five sessions, ground rules were made for discipline in the Hunter household. At the top of this list was the complete rejection of any physical form of punishment, including spanking. Erin and Joe could be reinforced for good behavior and could lose privileges for failure to adhere to house rules. In addition, it was agreed that Mrs. Hunter would quit her job and return to school. The Hunters agreed to discontinue their weekly restaurant trips and to buy cheaper clothing while Mrs. Hunter completed her schooling. This process was facilitated by Mr. Hunter receiving a promotion and raise at the bank.

Once Mr. Hunter returned to the home, therapy sessions continued for the next six months. Although tension increased when Mrs. Hunter returned to college in the fall, Mr. Hunter and the children reported no abusive incidents. Therapy was discontinued at the end of Mrs. Hunter's first semester in college.

The Department of Child Welfare completed a home evaluation one year later, before closing the Hunters' case. The social worker reported that Erin and Joe were happy and healthy. Both children were earning As in school and their teachers reported no bruises or unusual comments. Mrs. Hunter had continued her college education and was beginning to teach in the schools as part of her training. Mr. Hunter had steadily progressed at the bank. In addition, he had begun exercising at a local gym three nights a week. No further action was taken by the Department of Child Welfare.

References

ALLEN, A. J., LEONARD, H., & SWEDO, S. E. (1995). Current knowledge of medications for the treatment of childhood anxiety disorders. *Journal of the American Academy of Child and Adolescent Psychiatry, 34,* 976–986.

Diagnostic and Statistical Manual of Mental Disorders (1994). American Psychiatric Association.

DULCAN, M. K., BREGMAN, J. D., WELLER, E. B., & WELLER, R. A. (1995). Treatment of childhood and adolescent disorders. In A. F. Schatzberg & C. B. Nemeroff (Eds.) *Textbook of Psychopharmacology.* Washington, D.C.: American Psychiatric Press, pp. 669–706.

ENGELAND, H. V. (1993). Pharmacotherapy and behavior therapy: Competition or cooperation? *Acta Paedopsychiatrica International Journal of Child and Adolescent Psychiatry, 56,* 123–127.

FIXSEN, D. L., WOLF, M. M., & PHILLIPS, E. L. (1973). Achievement place: A teaching-family model of community-based group homes for youth in trouble. In L. Hammerlynck, L. Handy, and E. Mash (Eds.), *Behavior change: Methodology, concepts and practice.* Champaign, IL: Research Press.

GOULD, S. J. (1981). *The mismeasure of man.* New York: W. W. Norton.

HAROIAN, L. M. (1992). Sexual problems of children. In C. E. Walker, and M. C. Roberts (Eds.), *Handbook of Clinical Child Psychology.* New York: Wiley, pp. 431–450.

JONES, D. P. H. (1987). The untreatable family. *Child Abuse & Neglect, 11,* 409–420.

KAZDIN, A. E. (1995). Child, parent, and family dysfunction as predictors of outcome in cognitive-behavioral treatment of antisocial children. *Behaviour Research and Therapy, 33,* 271–281.

LOVAAS, O. J., & SMITH, T. (1989). A comprehensive behavioral theory of autistic children: Paradigm for research and treatment. *Journal of Behavior Therapy and Experimental Psychiatry, 20,* 17–29.

MORRIS, S., ALEXANDER, J. F., & WALDRON, H. (1988). Functional family therapy: Issues in clinical practice. In I.R.H. Fallon (Ed.), *Handbook of behavioral family therapy.* New York: Guilford.

NEISEN, J. D. (1992). Gender identity disorder of childhood: By whose standard and for what purpose? A response to Rekers and Morey. *Journal of Psychology and Human Sexuality, 5,* 65–67.

REID, W. H. (1989). *The treatment of psychiatric disorders.* New York: Bruner/Mazel.

REKERS, G. A. (1975). Stimulus control over sex-typed play in cross-gender identified boys. *Journal of Experimental Child Psychology, 20,* 136–148.

SEINFELD, J. (1989). Therapy with a severely abused child: An object relations perspective. *Clinical Social Work Journal, 17,* 40–49.

YARBROUGH, E., SANTAT, U., PEREL, I., & WEBSTER, C. (1987). Effects of fenfluramine on autistic individuals residing in a state developmental center. *Journal of Autism and Developmental Disorders, 17,* 303–314.

Index